Promise Lost

Promise Lost

Stephen Joyner, The Marine Corps, and the Vietnam War

Semper Fidelis,

Dan Moore

DAN MOORE

Hidden Shelf Publishing House
100 Abingdon Place, Abingdon, VA 24211
www.hiddenshelfbooks.com

Cover design: Allison Kaukola (niece of Stephen Joyner)
www.akgraphicdesigns.com

Cover photos courtesy of:
1) San Diego State University Athletics, 2) Bob Barnas
Author photo on back: Tobin Vaughn (SDSU)

Library of Congress Cataloging-in-Publication Data

Moore, Dan
Promise Lost:
Stephen Joyner, the Marine Corps, and the Vietnam War

ISBN: 1539676560
ISBN-13: 9781539676560

Printed in the United States of America

Table of Contents

To our brothers,
Sons of the Greatest Generation,
All-Americans, unafraid to go, to win
Yet another contest for your side.
The ultimate game, this one played out
Not on fields at home,
But in verdant landscapes of a foreign land,
Where you took exit amidst our tears
And cast your names on a black granite wall.

— Dan Moore

Introduction

Vietnam, June 1968—seeking relief from 107 degrees with 95 percent humidity, I had taken a mid-day break from duty in the battery's Fire Direction Center.

Alone in the darkened bunker of the officer's hooch, I sat on my cot with the latest copy of *Stars and Stripes* newspaper. On the Armed Forces Radio, Linda Ronstadt and the Stone Poneys were singing "Different Drum." Always a priority for anyone reading the paper, I scanned the list of servicemen recently killed.

Stephen Douglass Joyner . . . the name came like a blow to the gut. Stunned and speechless, I sat frozen, sick to my stomach, unable to speak, to cry, to process the news. My best friend gone.

———

Marines are trained to regard mission first and foremost. In combat, we have to move beyond the death of someone close to us, to focus on the job at hand.

For that reason, most American servicemen in Vietnam tried to avoid getting too familiar with each other. We might have been willing to lay down our lives for our fellow brothers-in-arms, but we hesitated to make friendships, to know too much about the other guy. We understood that anyone could be snatched away in an instant. But in truth, everyone struggled with losing someone they were close to in combat. Grief could be near impossible to suppress.

My assistant forward observer, Lance Corporal Ken Stetson, had died in the battle of Hue, now Steve Joyner. Within four months, both had been taken.

For years after Steve's death, I could not shake an unrelenting anguish mixed with anger and a crippling unfairness. I now grasped what every veteran of combat realizes at some point—war is a personal hell. Steve lost his life before he had a chance to live it. I had pledged in June 1968 that once I had the opportunity to record his life, I would do it.

———

In 2014, following my retirement from the CIA and after drafting an account of my own year in Vietnam for my family, I started to fulfill my distant promise to document Steve Joyner's life. I had no idea where the effort would lead me, but I plunged ahead. I felt qualified to recount his experience. I had a doctorate in history and experience using oral history to construct a complicated story. As Marine officers in Vietnam, we had shared similar experiences even though we were assigned to different divisions in I Corps—he in the Third Marine Division and me in the First Marine Division. Perhaps most important, I knew him personally.

My research on Steve has taken numerous unexpected turns, a few dead ends, and many diversions as pieces of his story have fallen into place. Because I had to learn Steve's view of the world, along with what he did in Vietnam, at times I felt like I had intruded into the private details of his all too brief life.

What began as a project to document the life of someone I viewed as a flawless Marine officer evolved gradually into a far different picture. I encountered a more nuanced and complex individual. As I gradually assembled information, Steve emerged as much more human than the "near-perfect Marine" I had always envisioned. Kaaren Joyner Page considered her younger brother to be "just a regular guy." Yes, he was that, but so much more.

Thanks to Kaaren, I obtained copies of letters he had written to her and their mother, most of them from Vietnam. The letters formed the foundation of a chronological narrative and an intriguing view of the war through his eyes.

Data points merged and occasionally conflicted. I conducted extensive phone interviews and received email input from Steve's relatives, friends, and colleagues from various stages of his life. Kaaren obtained her brother's Marine Corps personnel records. Added together, these sources for the most part provided a clear, coherent, and consistent picture of his character, personality, and relationships. Still, I sometimes had to make inferences and assumptions about Steve, while keeping an open mind and weighing disparate pieces of information.

The Joyner story has three voices—Steve's through his letters, the collective accounts of people who knew him, and my personal recollection of a month spent with him in 1968. While integrating the three sources to the extent possible, I have minimized secondary, collateral and background information except when and where they directly impact his life story.

Lieutenant Joyner's almost 50 letters form the linear core of the story from fall 1966—when he started Marine Corps officer training—to days before he fell in battle on 15 June 1968. The letters provide valuable insight into his values and the close and supportive family dynamic that sustained him.

On the whole, the letters are similar to those written home by other Vietnam servicemen: descriptive of the environment early in the tour, evolving over time into minimalist accounts of daily duties and, toward the end, pining for contact with family and anticipating a return to home and loved ones. For the most part, Steve avoided disturbing his family with graphic accounts of battles, certainly hoping to spare them from worry or alarm. A few letters reveal a glimpse of his shock and revulsion to the destruction of combat he witnessed. Whatever his deepest private concerns or fears might have been—with possible death no doubt a primary factor—he kept positive.

Steve's early letters from Vietnam provide the most detail about the combat environment. He described his surroundings, his daily routine, and on occasion, wrote about his concerns.

He noted the lack of small creature comforts, but he did not complain or dwell on physical deprivation. On different occasions, he requested a sweatshirt, socks, a pillowcase, a bed sheet, Kaaren's home-baked cookies.

As time passed, punctuated descriptions of events around him dwindled. Combat grew more intense, his duties more urgent and time consuming. A platoon commander for a brief six weeks, Steve assumed executive officer duties in early January 1968. In late May and early June, he acted as company commander. In time, perhaps to reduce the chaos and stress of combat around him, he allowed himself to dream of better times to come. His letters to family began to focus on what he would do once in their company again.

He was a master letter writer. Themes that recur in his letters provide insights to his perspective, underscoring his love of family and his enduring faith. He contemplated marriage upon returning home.

He expressed pride in wearing the uniform and the hard-earned honor of leading Marines in combat. He took a personal interest in and identified with his men, knew their full names, felt responsible for their welfare, and believed his role as an infantry officer in combat represented the crowning achievement of all that he had done in the Marine Corps.

In his letters, Steve never doubted the reasons for America's involvement in Vietnam. He did not openly question the utility of his mission, the policy aims of the U.S. government, or the goals of the Marine Corps in Vietnam.

He believed his transition from platoon commander to executive officer enhanced his value to the Corps and the war effort, making him a better Marine officer and a better person. In his last letters he did not allude to any danger that lay ahead.

In researching this project, nearly half a century after his passing, I discovered two distinct and at times conflicting views of Steve. He lived his 24 years in two seemingly similar, but in fact far different worlds: organized football through college and the Marine Corps during wartime. Each required special talents and skills, attributes that might appear to be interchangeable—teamwork, esprit de corps, discipline.

Friends from his pre-Marine Corps years can still describe with clarity and conviction his personality and accomplishments. With nearly every interview, a handful of detailed memories regarding what Steve said or did stood out. Each time it showcased something about his character or values. Above all, uncompromising personal integrity came to the fore. They remembered his athletic prowess, his total dedication to the team effort. Steve emerged as a straightforward, uncomplicated personality, an extrovert who never met a stranger. They noted his consistent ability to connect with others. They described an optimistic person who had faith in the future—a product of mid-century California culture and its seeming endless possibilities.

Marines who knew Steve viewed him through a different prism, one that placed less value on character and personality and more on competence in the field and officer leadership. In officer training at Quantico, his physical fitness most impressed those who knew him. He received high marks in graded physical endurance.

After leaving the Marine Corps officer training environment, the personal and character traits that stood Steve in a good stead as a college athlete and a friend to everyone who met him became less important. His military peers and seniors placed a high premium on subjective values—presence of mind, judgment, command presence, and other intangible, often subjective categories found on a Marine Corps officer's fitness report. More senior, career officers—some of whom doubtless viewed themselves as gatekeepers to the professional Marine Corps regular officer cadre—arguably placed the bar high for reserve, junior officers like Lt. Joyner.

Comments from enlisted Marines who knew Lt. Joyner in Vietnam focused for the most part on his concern for them and his ability to relate well to Marines under his command. While subordinates were divided on his leadership qualities in the field, they recalled his undeniable courage, dedication, energy, and decency.

On the whole, interviewed Marines were quite helpful, but at times guarded. Some seemed suspicious of my research, wanting to determine if I had a particular agenda. A few wondered why I had chosen to write the Joyner story. Had his life been more deserving of attention than others? A couple of Marines chose not to talk with me.

It is important to understand that adapting to life after serving in Vietnam has often been extremely difficult. Over the years, servicemen have had to deal with PTSD, alcoholism, and broken families. All of them are survivors.

Finally, there were my own memories of Vietnam. I arrived in Vietnam in August 1967. I was ready to serve my country, to do my best and to play a role in winning the war. But month by month, a sense of disillusionment began to fester and grow. Over time I found myself fighting two wars, the stark reality of Vietnam and the one inside my head.

Factors other than the loss of Joyner and Stetson were at work. I had gradually come to realize that the rural Vietnamese did not want Americans in their country. I had concluded that trying to win their hearts and minds had become futile.

I also grew aware of what I viewed as a chasm between junior Marine officers, who were mostly reservists, and the more senior professional officer cadre. I felt deep disappointment at times in what I viewed as blatant careerism and "ticket punching" of some officers and their occasional tactical decisions seemingly made without due regard for the safety of junior Marines.

Returning home, I remained in the U.S. Marine Corps Reserve after leaving active duty at the Marine Corps Recruit Training Regiment, Parris Island. I wanted to continue being a part of what I considered the best fighting force in existence and retain an association with the exemplary people who served in it. I valued the unique esprit de corps and camaraderie. I was proud of what I had done in Vietnam. I had shed too much sweat and too many tears to walk away from the Corps.

I tried for nearly 40 years, with mixed success, to limit negative memories of Vietnam. Raising a family and pursuing a career overseas helped push the war to the background of my consciousness. But it would not go away. I avoided discussing the war at length and could not read books or watch Hollywood films of the conflict. Researching and recording Steve's life has freed me from those bonds.

I have always felt that Steve's story needed to be told. It is a memorial to a beloved friend. I loved him as my brother. Had he survived Vietnam, he would have made an indelible, positive impact on so many other lives.

Besides detailing a fellow Marine's short but most honorable life, this story is also meant to be a tribute to the Vietnam generation of servicemen and women. They did not waver. They offered—and more than 58,000 gave—their lives for their country.

A Note From
Kaaren Joyner Page

P romise Lost is the story of my brother, Stephen Joyner. I caught waves with him on California beaches, attended his football games, danced to "I Can't Get No Satisfaction" at his college fraternity, nervously wrote and received countless letters from the battlefields of Vietnam, and brokenheartedly witnessed the draping of the red, white, and blue flag over his casket.

One

BEGINNINGS

In early March 1966, Steve Joyner took an oath that would alter the trajectory of his life. With pride and enthusiasm, he enlisted in the United States Marine Corps. Upon graduation from San Diego State College, he would report to Officer Candidates School in Quantico, Virginia.

The decision had been carefully formulated, the Marines having been on Steve's radar since the end of the 1965 Aztec football season. Until then, his options seemed consistent with his dreams ...possibly play pro football or begin a career in coaching.

But still trying to process the recent death of his father, Steve felt compelled to reorder his priorities. To his thinking, the welfare of his mother was now his responsibility. It was critical to make mature decisions. After long consideration and research, he welcomed military service. He believed the nation needed him.

Several weeks before signing the documents to join the Marines, he wrote to his older sister, Kaaren:

> The United States Marines are going to have my services for the next three years. Kaaren, this is not really so bad, as a matter of fact, it is great! My Officer Candidates School class will start the 22nd of August, with ten weeks of "basic" and I will become a first lieutenant in 18 months. One good factor is that I will play football on the Quantico base team and have all special services. After my three-year obligation, under the new GI Bill, the government will pay me for the next three years of education = teacher's credential, masters, etc.

Steve's plans came like a bolt out of the blue to his family and friends. The dramatic intensification of the war in Vietnam ignited their concern. Most were stunned, perplexed. While striving to understand his reason for joining the Marines, some of his family made a half-hearted effort to challenge the decision. His mother worried that he would face combat. She knew him well enough, however, not to question his decision. Kaaren had issues with the Vietnam War policy of the Johnson Administration, but knew it would be fruitless to try to convince him not to join the Marines. Younger sister June Ann recalled that Stephen told the family he wanted to serve his country and no one could really take exception to that sentiment. Cousin Kjell Kling asked him at a family gathering if he was sure he wanted to join the service. The answer: an emphatic but good-natured "Yes."

Most of Steve's Aztec teammates figured that the transition from collegiate football to the Marine Corps would be a natural fit. "He was gung-ho, like a Marine," said linebacker Cliff Kinney. "The kind of guy who would be inspirational as a leader." They also realized the difficulty Steve might have in leaving a sport that he had worked so hard to master, a game he had played with such passion and love. While not quite the size of a typical pro defensive end, he had the talent and makeup to be a game-changer as a special teams player. If not drafted by either the AFL or NFL, he could certainly be signed as a free agent. Coach Al Davis of the Oakland Raiders had sent him a letter requesting he keep the AFL franchise in mind. Had Steve decided to continue in football as a pro, the Raiders or any other team would have worked to place him in a National Guard or reserve unit, thereby eliminating the prospect of serving in Vietnam.

Adding to his options to continue in football after graduation, both of his college coaches—Don Coryell (San Diego State) and Hal Sherbeck (Fullerton Junior College)—had offered him coaching positions. If he stayed at San Diego State, he could start as a graduate assistant while earning his teaching credential.

Fraternity brothers at Sigma Phi Epsilon seemed staggered by the news. Most were trying to stay as far from South Vietnam as possible. Like everyone else, they had assumed that Steve would stay with football. There were plenty of theories why he chose the Marine Corps. Hil Contreras figured Steve joined the Corps for the same reason he loved football and fraternity life—brotherhood and teamwork. Bob Hood believed that the Marines appealed to Steve's desire to be a leader in what he considered the best fighting force in the U.S. military. Steve had several times talked at length about the Corps with Hood's father, who had been a Marine in World War II. Hood thought Joyner joined the Corps not to kill people or to experience combat, but for a more idealistic notion of helping win the war in Vietnam.

Some fraternity brothers talked to Joyner and tried to understand his decision, if not change his mind. They feared for his future. They thought he might not return from Vietnam. If the way he played football was any indication, he just might be too aggressive . . . going into battle without regard for his personal safety, "leading the charge" while placing himself at grave risk.

Still, beyond all the questioning and hand-wringing of family and friends, there was another possibility behind Steve's decision. Was service to his country imprinted in his DNA? Was he destined from birth to be a Marine?

———

On October 26, 1943, Stephen Douglass Joyner entered the world at the Our Lady of Angels Hospital in Hollywood, California. The second of Steve and June Joyner's three children, Stephen would be blessed with a close and loving family. Healthy, strong, and energetic, the boy steadily developed a set of impressive character traits—kindhearted, generous, happy . . .

In fact, a long list of advantages—none having to do with financial wealth—would help create an idyllic childhood.

Growing up in East Los Angeles and Orange County during an era when kids could freely explore a pristine, quasi-rural landscape in near perfect weather certainly proved beneficial. But most important in the formation of his personality and values was Stephen's family. Sixteen months older than her brother, Kaaren watched over him and he in turn worshipped her. Stephen's parents, moreover, would provide the strong emotional support and encouragement that would mold his character.

Stephen and parents in 1943

B orn in 1917, Homer Douglass Joyner, had grown up in York, Pennsylvania, where high school classmates nicknamed him "Steve." A superb student-athlete, the senior class president and valedictorian moved to California with an athletic scholarship from Fullerton Junior College (FJC). A basketball powerhouse, Fullerton won the state junior college championship in the 1938-39 season.

While at FJC, Steve met and fell in love with his future wife, June Foss. She and her Norwegian-American farming family had moved to Los Angeles several years earlier from Aberdeen, South Dakota.

Steve Joyner's success at Fullerton led to a basketball scholarship in 1939 to Loyola University in Los Angeles. But his main concern turned to June, expressing wonder in a love letter that she had agreed to marry "a character like me with only 75 cents to my name and not even knowing where my next nickel was coming from."

After their marriage in 1941, Steve left the university to work as a conductor for the Santa Fe Railroad. Without resources or savings, Steve and June struggled financially in the early years of their marriage. It didn't seem to matter.

They found an apartment in East Los Angeles at the new Wyvernwood garden complex. About three miles from the Los Angeles Union Station, the Federal Housing Administration-insured apartment project provided middle-income workers easy access to downtown L.A. and the nearby industrial centers.

During World War II, because the railroad was a critical transportation sector needed to move troops and materiel around the country, Steve was exempt from the draft and military duty. Early in his career, he traveled about 75,000 miles per year, taking him away from home for days at a time when the Joyner children were young.

"You have given birth to two of the most wonderful, intelligent, and best looking children," he wrote June on their fifth anniversary. "You have been a wonderful mother, and we have every right to be so proud of them. They have made a wonderful dream come true for me."

Stephen and Kaaren

To distinguish him from his father's nickname, the son would always be called "Stephen" by his family. When he started school, however, he would become and remain "Steve" to friends and classmates.

In summer, Kaaren and Stephen would walk to the nearby Lou Costello Foundation Youth Center, participating in day camps and learning to swim. According to Kaaren, interaction with the college student instructors made a lasting impression on the Joyner children.

After work, when their father wasn't traveling, he would often play catch with the children, including neighborhood kids, in the large grassy area in front of the apartment. Neighbors remembered Mr. Joyner as "a big man, gregarious, loving and generous . . . a caring father with great parental skills." Young

Stephen, like his father, had an outsized personality, both sharing a zest for life. The boy idolized his dad.

———

Mid-century Southern California seemed an ideal place for a family with children, where outside activity was a major part of life from sunup to sundown. Always active, the family often took the train from Fullerton to the San Diego Zoo or headed to the beach where the kids played with rented rafts or body surfed. The family enjoyed hiking and camping in state and national parks, occasionally sharing a mountain cabin with friends during the winter.

Four years old

Several times the Joyner family rode cross-country on the train for summer vacations in South Dakota and Pennsylvania. Kaaren recalled that her father "would get off the train and hurriedly buy bread, cold cuts and cheese and make sandwiches for everyone in our railroad car. At night he would spread newspapers over us to keep us warm. That's how my dad was: no money, but he made it fun and always shared with others."

The birth of their third child, June Ann in 1948, along with Steve's new job working on freight trains out of

Fullerton, prompted the parents to consider buying a home. In 1951, Steve and June found a great location in the northern Orange County suburb of La Habra, purchasing a new three-bedroom, one-bathroom home within a cul-de-sac on North Valencia Street.

Built on former orange groves with surrounding farmland, the La Habra sub-division retained its semi-rural flavor throughout the 1950s—a safe and pleasant community whose citizens mostly shared the same middle class values and aspirations. Many of the families were young, providing the three Joyner siblings the ability to play and explore in a neighborhood filled with children. With only a 15-minute commute to work, Steve could be home nearly every afternoon to spend time with the kids.

As a boy, an energetic Stephen loved sports, playing in the cul-de-sac with his friends, and delivering papers for the *La Habra Star*. His older sister described him as fun, loving and helpful at home, always doing his chores without fail. Stephen struck one neighbor as "gentle and sweet, nice to everyone." A cousin recalled that Stephen always seemed happy and went out of his way to be kind and inclusive with younger children, involving them in conversations when other older kids ignored them. He loved telling funny stories to them. He also looked after his younger sister, June Ann.

Like numerous other families in the neighborhood, the Joyners kept to a tight budget. Steve received a paycheck from the railroad twice a month. Homemaker June, a good cook, managed to put plenty of food on the table. Always driving a used car, neither parent placed great value on material things. Yet the Joyner children felt no sense of deprivation, even though Stephen was a notorious "big eater." With the bimonthly pay cycle, the children joked that they ate steak one week and beans the next, although years later Kaaren could not recall having steak.

Both Steve and June Joyner valued public service, believing that responsible people gave back to the community. A founding member of the Fullerton Elks Lodge in 1956, Steve would eventually become its Exalted Ruler in 1964-65. He was also active in the Yorba Linda Masons, the Railway Union, and the Sons of Norway.

Steve placed a premium on family values. He lived the Elks mission of service—belief in God, charity, justice, brotherly love, fidelity, patriotism, and benevolence. Steve Joyner passed these ideals on to his children, always instilling in them to be the best they could be. He prepared his children for life.

As dedicated to community involvement as her husband, June Joyner at various times served as a trustee of the La Habra elementary school district, a PTA president, treasurer of the Orange County school board association, and a director of the California school board association. She later became active in Democratic Party politics, focused on education issues.

Exemplifying 1950s America, the Joyner family members were products of a certain culture and background. Many of their friends were World War II veterans. Some were first or second generation Americans. Understandably, a strong sense of patriotic pride—of God and Country—permeated their daily lives, passed down from parent to child.

Assimilating lessons learned from their parents, the Joyner children aspired to become moral beacons by living lives of integrity and compassion. "We were instilled with the fact that when we left the house we all represented the Joyner family," Kaaren remembered. "Anything we did as individuals, good or bad, reflected on the family. So we were sure it was always positive."

———

With their many civic connections, Steve and June enjoyed a wide circle of friends outside of their close-knit neighborhood. They also had a large extended family. June's father and brother lived in the area, as did her sisters, cousins, and their children. Steve's family and friends in Pennsylvania kept in touch and occasionally visited.

Get-togethers at the Joyner home often included music and dancing, the popular family striking everyone as both nurturing and lively. Stephen's cousins remembered that the joyful, noisy Joyner household seemed filled with relatives, all of whom enjoyed one another's company.

"The children were surrounded by truly happy people who always had time for us, made us laugh, and encouraged us how to enjoy life," recalled Cousin Marty Morgen.

In his early teens, Stephen began to turn into an entertainer. All three cousins—Gil Warren, Marty, and Stephen—attended the 1957 Boy Scout Jamboree in Valley Forge, Pennsylvania. According to Cousin Gil, Stephen had become a "magnet, a big clown that everyone liked to be around." Somewhere along the line, friends nicknamed him Goofy.

Stephen c. 1958

While a future career as a comedian may have been a possibility, Stephen's chief focus became organized sports. An average student academically, he participated in track, basketball, and football. As he grew, he gravitated toward football, his quickness and strength immediately catching the attention of coaches.

Along with athletic prowess, his beaming and extroverted personality helped make him a favorite among students. During a time when a popular teen's social contacts were often limited to those deemed as belonging to the "cool" crowd, Steve enjoyed the company of girls and boys across the entire high school socio-economic spectrum.

Two

An Athlete Emerges

Steve Joyner seemed born to play football. Strong and athletic, he possessed that perfect mixture of enthusiasm, fortitude, and talent. He reveled in the camaraderie. At La Habra High School, he excelled at defensive end and middle linebacker. For good measure, he was also an outstanding offensive end for the Highlanders.

Although he participated in varsity basketball and track, football was his game. His passion and "never-say-die" approach on the field made him a perennial favorite of coaches and teammates. He also was growing in size and strength. During the summer before his junior year, Steve spent two weeks at Camp Pendleton Marine Base in the Devil Pups program for young teenagers.

After the 1959 football season, his coaches selected him as both the most improved and best defensive player.

By his senior year in 1960, Steve had become a football star and "big man on campus." Teammates selected Steve and lineman Pat Moretta as co-captains. "Steve was lively with a whole lot of energy," said Moretta. "He had a great sense of humor."

Joyner was also intense. Always positive with a flair for the dramatic, he urged the Highlanders to break huddles in a serpentine formation similar to that used by UCLA at the time. Steve treated teammates with great respect, pumping them up when they were down and going out of his way not to hurt others to get the job done on the field. Even so, he could become unsettled when he encountered a defeatist attitude on a team that did not have an abundance of skilled players.

It was not uncommon, at that time, for coaches to discipline players with force. One afternoon the head coach asked his assistant coach to get out the paddle. Lining up the players, the reluctant assistant coach, as he always did, used just enough power for the head coach in the other room to hear the pop. He gave the imposing Joyner a restrained tap. "Is that all you've got?" said Steve. With no other choice but to lose face in front of the team, the assistant pulled the paddle back, took a batter's stance, and gave it all he had.

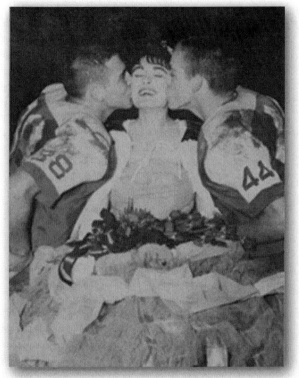

Co-Captains Steve Joyner (R) and Pat Moretta (L) plant
a surprise kiss on Homecoming Queen Jacque Cothran,
who portrayed Snow White at Disneyland.

Despite missing a good portion of his senior season due to
a leg injury, coaches elected Joyner to the Orange County all-
star football game. Playing against a South County team that
featured John Huarte, the future Heisman Trophy winner for
the University of Notre Dame, Steve was having no success
tackling the prize quarterback. At one point, a frustrated and
emotional Joyner returned to the North County's defensive

huddle with tears in his eyes, telling his teammates that despite his best efforts, he simply could not bring the quarterback down.

Even so, the football community in the region regarded Joyner as one of the top players in La Habra High School history.

"He was fun to be with, easy going and full of life," said La Habra quarterback David Veatch. "Big and tough and a great target to throw to. God didn't make people any better than Steve."

While enjoying the companionship on the football team, Steve also celebrated victories with the student body. Classmate Judy Fischle emphasized how much the football star was admired: "He had such a good spirit and was always so nice to everyone, except those on opposing football teams."

Barbara Anderson, a cheerleader who briefly dated Steve in high school, found him an "atypical jock" . . . he had no ego. His solid relationships with people stood out. "He had a big heart, not a big head."

Faith became an integral part of Steve's character. At a young age, he came under the influence of "Grandma Wilson," a deeply religious neighbor who had two grown daughters and treated him as she would a grandson. At about age 15, Steve began to visit First Yorba Linda Friends Church with his cousin Gil Warren. It had a much different energy than he had experienced at the local Methodist Church the Joyner family occasionally attended. The large, lively, and active teen group at the Friends

Church appealed to him. He loved the music and, yes, the large number of attractive girls. Once he obtained his driver's license, Steve began attending weekly services, joining the youth choir and church basketball team.

Still, football remained the all-encompassing focal point of Steve's life, and it would become a bridge to higher education. While his intellectual curiosity would continue to build, academics always took a back seat to sports. With report cards that hovered just above average, Steve chose to attend junior college while living at home.

To sharpen his grades, Steve decided to sit out the 1961 football season at Fullerton JC. With a major in physical education and minor in architectural engineering, he seemed to have aspirations of someday becoming a teacher and coach.

But he did not spend all his time locked in studies. Under the guidance of athletic trainer Bill Chambers, Steve worked hard to enhance his already powerful frame. Chambers, who described Steve as a "rare physical specimen," remembered his strength and unquestioning dedication.

More than that, Chambers admired Steve's character and integrity, describing him as always positive and cheerful, giving back ten-fold in every relationship. Along with that came a tendency to willingly accept a teammate's word. If misled, Steve expressed disappointment rather than anger that a person would betray his trust.

—

Entering the 1962 season, Joyner had already become a favorite of the entire Fullerton coaching staff.

"He's a tough kid on the field, but a nice person off," Coach Hal Sherbeck told a reporter for the *Los Angeles Times*. "I wish I had a whole team of Steve Joyners."

For starters, Steve and his coach shared near exact character traits. Sherbeck, in his second year at Fullerton, had already earned a reputation as a caring and compassionate coach who held his players to the highest standards of excellence in all aspects of their lives while stressing a positive mental outlook.

Naturally, Steve followed coaching instruction without question, a characteristic he carried for all authority figures.

Attending Fullerton turned out to be an excellent choice, as he played for a man who would become one of junior college football's legendary coaches. In 31 seasons at Fullerton (1961-91), Hal Sherbeck compiled a 240-70-8 record while coaching the Hornets to three national championships. He had but one losing season, in 1963, Steve's last at the school.

Loaded with talent in 1962, the Hornets finished with a 6-2-1 record, ranked 24th in the nation in the junior college polls, and produced four honorable mention All-Americans—quarterback Brig Owens, halfback John Pease, offensive guard Gene Keeler, and defensive end Steve Joyner.

Owens, who described Steve as his closest friend on the Hornets team, headed for the University of Cincinnati after finishing at Fullerton. He would become an All-American quarterback there and would spend 12 years as one of the all-time great safeties of the Washington Redskins.

While noting that Steve "could do anything on the football field," Owens lauded his hyper and spirited personality. "Always laughing, a life force, a heck of an athlete."

Bound for stardom at the University of Utah, John Pease would coach football for 40 years, including 19 in the NFL with the New Orleans Saints and Jacksonville Jaguars. He retired in 2016 as the defensive coordinator at Utah.

Pease described Steve as one of the most focused players he had ever known, dedicated to personal excellence on the field and to his teammates. "Joyner had high moral standards," Pease said, "a well-grounded person comfortable with his own ethical code."

While opposing coaches praised Joyner's skills on offense and defense, he also had an avid fan base, including his former high school principal. Walter Pray wrote a letter congratulating Steve for his sportsmanship and "clean, hard-hitting brand of football." Pray closed with encouragement: "Hit those books, Steve, you can have a fine career."

Prior to Steve's All-America honors, Orange County sports-writers selected him as first team all-conference defensive end. He was also voted by his teammates as Most Inspirational Player and the coaches named him the Hornets' Outstanding Lineman.

Following the '62 season, even though he still had a year of JC eligibility, Joyner attracted the attention of numerous football programs eager to enroll him. The University of Washington, Long Beach State, Idaho State, University of Tulsa, and Florida State were in the early hunt. Joyner showed polite interest, but did not commit.

Football recruiters from Brigham Young University came to Fullerton to meet with Owens and Joyner. Once the recruiters realized Owens was African-American, however, they dropped contact with the quarterback. Angry and disappointed at BYU's treatment of Owens, Steve eliminated them from consideration.

When Owens arrived at Cincinnati, he helped Steve set up a trip to Ohio to look at the program. Owens thought the visit went well. He knew the coaching staff wanted Joyner to play football there. After the visit, Steve told his friend and former teammate that he had been impressed with the Bearcats' program and submitted an application for admission, but soon lost interest. Owens thought that perhaps Steve's sister, Kaaren, had weighed in to convince him to attend a college closer to home.

Actually, Steve had his eyes on another program. In the summer of '63, San Diego State College had joined the recruiting mix. Aztec coach Don Coryell established contact with him through Hal Sherbeck. Both charismatic and vibrant personalities, Sherbeck and Coryell were built from the same mold—outstanding coaches with deep empathy for their players.

While some schools would have gladly welcomed Joyner for the fall season, Coryell discouraged him from leaving Fullerton before his second year of playing. In a letter inviting Steve and his parents to visit the SDSC campus, Coryell said he hoped Steve would be playing for Coach Sherbeck in the fall and then come to SDSC in the spring.

He reminded Steve that "education is the most important thing in your life at this time" and when the Aztecs two starting ends graduated after the upcoming season "we would like to have you step in and take their place." Coryell had big dreams. "Our football program is on the way up," he told Steve. "By the time you graduate, we plan to be able to hold our own with the major colleges in the nation."

Steve took Coryell's advice and stayed at Fullerton, telling a journalist that he had planned only to play JC football for one season before transferring to a four-year college. Instead, he explained, he liked Fullerton enough to stay for two. The article in the *Los Angeles Times* was titled "Choir Boy Tough Guy on College Gridiron."

In a surprise lackluster 1963 season, the Hornets suffered five early hard-luck losses before rebounding for a 3-5-1 record. Again, it would be Coach Sherbeck's only losing season at Fullerton.

Sherbeck noted that Joyner was such a tough competitor that he had a hard time shrugging off defeat, sometimes crying in the locker room. But on the field, Steve excelled in every game, building his skillset and burnishing his reputation as a genuine star. While playing both defense and offense, Steve told a reporter, "I'd rather play defense, it's more natural for me. Defense is mostly reaction. On offense I have to be thinking all the time."

The program for the Grossmont College game in November 1963 noted: "Coaches throughout the Conference have labeled him one of the finest all-around ends the Eastern Conference has ever seen. Certainly, Joyner will be rated one of the all-time greats in half a century of football at FJC."

At the end of the season, Steve Joyner was selected first team Junior College All-America as a defensive end. He also won first team all-conference honors for the second year in a row. His coaches named him the team's Most Valuable Player. Even his mother was recognized for her support of the Hornets.

Steve receives Fullerton JC "Athlete of the Year" Award.

Joyner was named the school's overall "Athlete of the Year" and one of the 25 FJC campus "Men of Distinction." He also received the Arthur L. Nunn Memorial Award as the "Most Inspirational Athlete of the Year" based on his "leadership qualities, athletic success, and academic success."

Steve's next step would be San Diego State College, having accepted a strong financial aid offer to play for the Aztecs. The football world seemed to be opening up to him.

Three

SAN DIEGO STATE

B y recruiting top prospects from the junior college ranks, Don Coryell had begun to build a Division II powerhouse at San Diego State. His teams were noted for explosive passing, quickness on both sides of the ball, and winning. His personal philosophy—which never faltered—emphasized determination, moral fortitude, and a love for people. His staff included future NFL Hall of Fame coaches John Madden and Joe Gibbs. The program, school, location—to Steve, it could not have been a more perfect fit.

With solid and wide-ranging academics, SDSC enrolled about 15,000 students in the mid-1960s, mostly high-achieving undergraduate commuters from all over San Diego County. A short two-hour drive from La Habra, the beautiful campus of Spanish colonial architecture rests about 12 miles inland from the Pacific Ocean. In January 1964, Joyner matriculated in time for spring football.

A junior, he set his academic sights on majoring in Physical Education, a popular path for students interested in a coaching career. The program had an excellent reputation with a faculty that had done leading research in various fields of athletic training education.

San Diego State also had a reputation as a party school with a robust "Greek" presence. Barbara Anderson, who briefly dated Steve in high school and now attended SDSC, asked if he might be interested in joining a fraternity. With a positive response, she introduced him to members of Sigma Phi Epsilon.

Like most fraternities, Sig Ep contained many members serious about academics, but was essentially a social organization. That said, students generally regarded Sigma Phi Epsilon near the upper rung of SDSC fraternities in prestige.

"We valued having a varsity football player like Joyner in the fold," said Sig Ep Joe Sullivan. "His presence enhanced the status of the fraternity. He was a chick magnet."

Soon after Steve pledged in the spring of '64, fraternity president Vince Biondo asked why he did not choose Sigma Chi fraternity, where most of the football players gravitated. Joyner laughed and explained he hung around teammates enough every day at practice. "I'm not going to learn anything outside of football from most of those jocks," he explained to the Sig Ep president. "Here I can experience and enjoy college life as most regular guys do."

Steve reveled in life as a pledge. When an active member requested Pledge Joyner "give 15 pushups" for making a mistake reciting the Greek alphabet, Steve excitedly followed orders with not 15, but 100 pushups . . . half with his right behind the back and half with his left hand not touching the ground. Joyner's pushups quickly drew a huge crowd of brothers, cheers mixed with awe.

Finished with 100 and capable of much more, Steve got to his feet and faced the active brother who had given the order. "You better learn that alphabet," the active said, trying to keep a straight face. "Yes sir," replied Steve . . . and he did.

One by one, fraternity brothers painted the same portrait of Steve's personality—fun, focused, popular, positive, caring, generous. On one level, just an average guy who happened to play football. On another, a man of unquestioned integrity. He towered over many in the fraternity both in physical stature and in virtue, one fraternity brother recalled. A handshake from Steve Joyner was a virtual bond.

Bob Hood described Steve as a "transparent personality who took what people said to him at face value. He came across as a little gullible. He trusted people and avoided questioning anyone's integrity or motives without cause."

"He was an open book," said fraternity brother and roommate Wes Hills. "He did not hide his emotions." Hills added that Steve liked to party, but not to excess.

Steve also liked girls . . . for the right reasons. Ever the gentleman, Steve treated the women he dated with empathy and consideration in the same way he treated friends. In the eyes of some of his fraternity brothers, he appeared a bit old-fashioned and chivalrous.

Girls, however, appreciated his manners and were at ease with him. Cheerleader Dena Windsor Gillespie, one of Joyner's girlfriends during the 1964 football season, described him as "conscientious, intelligent, cute, amorous, and family-oriented." She trusted him because he respected women, due in large part, she thought, to the high regard he had for his mother and sisters. "He was not an animal" with one objective in mind.

Steve participated in fraternity activities when he found the time, but football took precedence. It began with spring football, the reason Steve transferred at mid-year.

Don Coryell preferred recruiting fast, athletic, and talented junior college standouts over incoming freshmen. Joyner fit the Coryell profile to a T.

It didn't take long for the Aztec football players to gravitate toward Steve's easy manner; impressed with his enthusiasm, intensity, dedication, and compassion. "He was genuine," said linebacker Cliff Kinney. "What you saw was what he was . . . excited about life and loved sharing his enthusiasm. He supported you on the field and was a friend to everyone on the team."

John Seebold, a fraternity brother and SDSC rugby player who worked out with the football team in the spring, said Steve "played full throttle with every play, but left his aggression on the playing field."

Four games into the 1964 season, Steve wrote a letter to his older sister, who had taken a teaching position in Northern California. He told Kaaren about his challenging classes and work-study in the Health Center, but was most excited that the Aztecs were undefeated.

Defensive coordinator John Madden gave Joyner the role of "forcer," a defensive end whose job involved disrupting plays and causing general chaos in the opponent's backfield. Steve did not disappoint. The coaches singled him out as a standout twice during the season, once against Los Angeles State, the number one small college team in the nation. Aztec coaches named Joyner the defensive star of the game against UC Santa Barbara, the media stating that he led a "charged-up defensive line on virtually every play."

Teammates called him "Peewee Panther," a variant of his childhood nickname, Peewee.

"He did whatever the coaches asked him to do and more," said Kinney.

1964 Aztec defensive starters included Joyner (37), Wayne Bienhoff (83), Ken Madison (82) and Jerry Koch (80).

Steve had always been deeply inspired by his coaches. Like Hal Sherbeck at Fullerton, Don Coryell represented a father figure. Steve often talked to a girlfriend about what the coach said and how he inspired the team. Steve respected Coryell's honesty, fairness, morals, sportsmanship, and demand for excellence—all qualities that Joyner's own friends saw in him.

The Aztecs would finish with an 8-2 record in '64, outscoring the opposition 423-71 and ranking in the top ten of the small college division.

Steve leavened his fierce competitive spirit on the gridiron with a generous dose of humor. Mike Gerry, a friend and varsity swimmer, lamented with Steve about an upcoming meet against Long Beach State star and Olympic Gold Medalist Gary Ilman. For Gerry to win the race, Joyner jokingly offered to "take care" of Ilman.

In a Kinesiology class his junior year at SDSC, Steve took exception to a statement by Dr. Fred Kasch, who, discussing exercise physiology, stated that athletes in strength sports such as football in general lacked the endurance capacity of athletes in sports such as swimming, rowing, cycling, and distance running. Kasch had done research work in exercise physiology to measure the intake of oxygen to test endurance capacity. Kasch told the class that he doubted any football player could break a minute in the 440-yard dash. To Kasch's surprise, Joyner stated that he could do it. After some good-natured back and forth, Kasch arranged for the class to join Steve on the track a few days later. With a backdrop of student cheers, Steve ran the 440 in something like 54 seconds, making the feat look routine.

———

At home for the Christmas break, Stephen was particularly excited to become a member of the Fullerton Elks, sponsored by his father Steve, the Exalted Ruler of the chapter. As they always had been, the two were extremely close; the son's character traits both inherited and copied from his father. Friends and relatives always chuckled at how each was a clone of the other.

"How far you go, progress or participate is strictly up you," wrote Stephen's dad in a newsletter to the Fullerton Elks membership. "Isn't this, then, like life in this great country of ours? When we are born the struggle begins. How far we travel, what road we take, is strictly up to us as individuals. The paths are many and varied but all lead to our ultimate goal if we strive hard enough."

In February 1965, while working at the Santa Fe Railway, Homer "Steve" Joyner died suddenly from a heart attack. He was only 47 years old.

Informed of what happened on a San Diego golf course, a devastated son dropped his club and left for La Habra.

———

How much his father's death directly affected his final year at SDSC and the decisions he made about his future cannot be determined with certainty, but to some friends, Steve's goals in life seemed to change. Football became less important to him. Those around him still saw the drive and focus on the football field, but he appeared more subdued and serious. Steve informed one fraternity brother that the football grind sometimes wore him down. He told a girlfriend that his perspective had changed after his father's passing. He now thought of himself as the man of the family and felt a strong obligation to look after his mother.

Steve's senior football season was solid, although he often shared playing time. While a few fraternity brothers on occasion yelled in unison "Put Joyner in the game" from the stands, Steve showed no concern with his role on the team. He certainly would never question a coaching decision.

Overall, the '65 Aztec defense managed five shutouts as San Diego State compiled another 8-2 record while outscoring the opposition 353-87. What the "Aztecs of Montezuma Mesa" did not realize at the time was that their five wins to close the season would be the start of a 25-game winning streak, on the way to two national championships under Coach Coryell.

Before moving to the NFL, Don Coryell would coach the Aztecs for 12 seasons, posting a 104-19-2 record with three undefeated teams and propelling San Diego State University into big time Division I football.

Dan Moore

After the 1965 football season, PE department faculty member Dr. Carl Benton had rhetorically asked Steve and teammate Alan Duke what they planned to do upon graduation. Benton, a former Marine, suggested they consider military service to country, noting that he could help them get into the Marine Corps officer program. The idea appealed to Steve.

At the beginning of the spring semester, Steve heard that SDSC student Ross Brown had gone through the Marine Platoon Leaders Class (PLC) program and would be commissioned a Marine second lieutenant upon graduation in June. While the two had never met, Brown immediately recognized the prominent Aztec football player when answering the unexpected knock on his apartment door. Steve explained that he had not yet contacted a recruiter, but wanted to know what Brown thought of the Marine Corps and what his experiences had been in the PLC program.

They spoke for two hours, Brown describing to Joyner the details of his two intensive six-week sessions as an enlisted Marine and officer candidate during the summers after his sophomore and junior years. Steve appeared relaxed, pleasant, and listened intently. Brown gave him the name and phone number of the Marine Officer Selection Officer (OSO), the point of contact for graduating PLCs.

In late February, when Steve wrote the letter to his sister that he would be joining the Marine Corps, he first mentioned several other recent developments. The only bad news was that Jo had returned his fraternity pin. "She feels that we were really too serious and doesn't value 'the pin' as much as I do," he wrote Kaaren. "I have talked to her since she mentioned her feelings to me, but she wants to leave things 'normal' and 'still date' but no pin. I really don't have any security in this situation so we are no longer dating each other!"

Better news, he would definitely be graduating in June: "I feel great about this and just had to tell you."

Thrilled to have been elected Sigma Phi Epsilon athletic director, he didn't mention to his sister that upon his nomination, none of his fraternity brothers attempted to run against him.

———

SDSC senior classmate Joe Gerry—swimmer Mike Gerry's brother—met Steve in spring 1966 when they were working to get into shape for OCS, both adhering to a rigorous regime of weight training and running four miles per day. Gerry, who would attend Officer Candidates School (OCS) and The Basic School (TBS) with Steve, thought the former football star already looked like a Marine officer recruiting poster.

Meanwhile, six of Steve's teammates were selected in the 1966 pro football draft, including Cliff Kinney to the Raiders. Quarterback and Sig Ep fraternity brother Don Horn, a year behind Steve, would be the first pick of the Green Bay Packers the following season. Steve, of course, had already made his commitment.

After graduating from SDSC in June 1966, Steve charted a lengthy cross-country drive in his Volkswagen Bug with the ultimate destination of Quantico Marine Base in northern Virginia. After visiting his mother's side of the family in South Dakota, he headed for Pennsylvania to stay with relatives and friends of his father while working in construction and as a lifeguard at the York Boys Club until starting Officer Candidates School on 22 August 1966.

"He had this huge presence, both physically and in his personality," said Louanne Chilstrom, a family friend in York. "People gravitated to him."

In mid-August 1966, Joyner prepared to begin his training and notified friends and relatives how to contact him. In a letter to a married friend from Fullerton JC expecting her first child, Steve wished her all the best, noting that someday he hoped to have "a boy named Doug and a girl named Janice Marie."

Steve might have had matrimony on his mind. He had met Bev a month prior to graduation. "She lives in Pomona, CA and has one more year at SDSC," he wrote. "She is around 5

'5" and 120. Has green eyes with light brown hair that goes to her hips . . . I gave her my frat pin on July 4 and I really think this is the one. She is a good Christian girl."

Steve with Bev

Four

Officer Candidates School

O n 22 August 1966, Steve Joyner reported to the Marine Corps Base in Quantico, Virginia to begin a grueling 10-week course at the Marine Corps OCS. Arriving at Quantico by bus, train, and car, more than 800 men in the 41st Officer Candidate Course (OCC) reported for duty that would change their lives. They were issued utility uniforms and military gear and divided into 16 platoons of about 50 men each, four platoons per company. Enjoying a typical summer day of sweltering heat and high humidity, the new officer candidates were then marched to their barracks by staff platoon sergeants. The following day they had an intake physical exam and received their haircuts.

From the first day to the last, the OCS staff applied maximum physical and psychological stress on candidates to identify those who could not demonstrate the qualities required for com-missioning as a Marine Corps officer. Evaluations were based on four attributes—leadership, moral, mental, and physical. While those with enlisted Marine Corps military experience had an initial advantage, the intensive psychological and physical pressure soon leveled the playing field.

Endurance—the foundation of a candidate's evaluated performance—overshadowed all else. The OCS staff challenged candidates with a crushing repetition of forced marches, long distance runs in full military gear, the rugged combat obstacle and confidence courses, and other measures of fitness. The OCS staff assessed how each candidate handled the relentless stress and struggle, particularly the endurance tests, which could easily break a person who might excel in other areas. If a candidate fell short, he found himself before a staff performance board. While some dropped on request (DOR), others were deemed unfit to continue and pushed out. Overall, the attrition rate would be about 15 percent.

"I live with 50 other candidates in what is called a squad bay," Steve would write his sister. "These men are from all over the U.S. and hold degrees in every type of field. We go through a day which starts at 0530 and ends at 2200. The chow, food, is not bad, but you only have about 10 to 15 minutes to eat.

"That reminds me, everything we do is double-time. On the 'average' day we will start with physical fitness for one hour. After PT (physical training) and chow, we will either attend lectures in History, Drill, Camouflage, or Weapons. In the afternoon we will have more lectures and drill. Once a week we have a conditioning hike, which is around 10 miles, done in full gear!!"

Like most candidates, Joyner tried to avoid too much attention from punitive staff on the lookout for any weakness or notable pre-OCS activity they could leverage against him. His prominent gridiron experience, however, made that impossible. Word soon got out that Joyner had been a junior college All-American. The OCS staff began calling him "football head" and "football brain."

No matter, Marine Corps officer training seemed a natural fit for Joyner. He appeared "squared away" and coped well with whatever harassment the staff threw at him.

Joyner (4th from left, front) and his OCS platoon – Dress Right Dress, Field Day, 26 October 1966

Not surprising, Steve stood out in strength and endurance tests. The OCS staff used him as an example to demonstrate aggressive, self-confident approaches to the challenging obstacle course, the daily dozen physical training exercises, and how to approach endurance runs.

One candidate noted that Joyner's superb physical conditioning and above average height allowed him to set the pace for platoon conditioning runs. The long distance running configurations usually began in formation by tallest to shortest. Should a candidate begin to lag, the next in line would take his place, the well-conditioned Marines continually moving up in the order. Repeated instances of straggling could spell doom for candidates. For Joyner, falling behind was never a problem. Classmate Leroy Wilkerson remembered that he spent the entire OCS course looking at Joyner's back.

Steve excelled with the pugil stick, a heavily padded pole-like weapon used by Marines since World War II for rifle bayonet training. His sheer strength produced a string of impressive victories, the candidate's fearsome aggression prompting instructors to limit his activity out of concern he might injure someone. One classmate prayed for divine intervention that he would not have to enter the ring against the former SDSC football player.

Marion Sims, the eventual OCS class honor man and 60 pounds lighter, once faced Joyner in the pugil stick pit with much of the company in attendance. Based on what he had seen and heard about Joyner's prowess, Sims anticipated the worst. To his surprise, however, Joyner allowed him to stand toe-to-toe for several blows, a generous and appreciated gesture.

John Powell, who had won a lighter weight division, experienced something similar when forced to join Joyner in the ring. "I was pleased he didn't do permanent damage to me," said Powell, "and he even took a few lumps."

———————

In mid-September, Joyner received a letter from his mother. "Honey, I love you," wrote June Joyner, "and I really hope this life (at Quantico) isn't too tough on you." Tongue in cheek, she promised to call the President to complain if her son found OCS too demanding.

Joyner's adaption to OCS pressure impressed his contemporaries. With an admirable work ethic and drive to succeed, he always seemed prepared. Thomas Jauntig recalled watching what Steve did and tried to follow his lead. He noted that, without fanfare, Joyner often helped other candidates with difficult physical tasks.

Steve thrived on the OCS experience, its physical challenges and the camaraderie that must have reminded him of past football training camps.

"He really loved the Corps," said Jauntig. "No matter how hard it got, he always seemed to take it in stride and do what had to be done. He believed in himself, his ability spoke through his actions."

Candidate Joyner received a personal visit from Marine lieutenants' Ross Brown (from San Diego State) and Fred Meier (La Habra High) who had completed the course months before. When the sergeant on duty summoned him, Joyner showed up at the door of the staff office. Following multiple pushups at the sergeant's direction, the candidate and the lieutenants talked in a private meeting. While Brown urged Steve to play the OCS game—"Hang loose, say nothing, and do the job of getting through 10 weeks"—the candidate expressed enthusiasm about the training he had received. His strategy for completing OCS, the lieutenants discovered, did not include mere survival. He wanted to excel.

"Tomorrow we have a seven-mile hike with history classes in the afternoon," Steve wrote an uncle. "Next Monday we are to have a history exam, so the major part of my 'weekend' will be spent studying. I ordered my uniform for graduation, it cost $153!! But does it look sharp."

With little spare time, Steve managed to send his girlfriend, Bev, a greeting card showing a military brawl in a saloon with his written caption: "Just like the ole frat." He added his love for her and the Marine Corps training regimen, expressed compassion for a candidate who had washed out of the program, and noted that "adjusting to military life is tough for some, but not for me."

He also told Bev that he was far from being the perfect Marine: "At inspection yesterday, which I will never forget, I stood in full uniform, my brass gleaming, my hair trimmed, my shoulders back, my chest out, my stomach in, and my fly open!!"

Replying to a letter from Kaaren, Stephen mentioned that he had opened a bank account after receiving his first paycheck ($52) and thought very highly of his platoon commander, Captain William Stensland. "He is the one man who will make or break me in this program."

One other thing to his older sister: "In your letter, you asked me if I ever get a break . . . my answer is NEVER!!"

Joyner maintained his wit and positive attitude throughout OCS. Early in the training, he worked hard in the platoon squad bay to master the "About Face" drill movement. To the amusement of the platoon, he gave himself vocal orders over and over in front of a full-length mirror for twenty straight minutes until he had it perfected.

While Joyner respected and admired his staff platoon commander, it did not restrain him from poking fun at Capt. Stensland. One day in the squad bay with platoon candidates present, Joyner affected some of Stensland's mannerisms. While Joyner placed his hands in his belt and rocked on his heels, imitating Stensland's voice and inflection—all of which he had down pat—the captain walked in and observed the performance.

Feigning anger, Stensland called Joyner to his office for a private counseling session. The candidate emerged red faced and never said a word to members of the platoon about the discussion. It struck some platoon members that Stensland, in fact, had the greatest respect for Steve's dedication and commitment.

Late in the course, Steve received another brief note of strong encouragement from his mother asking about her "favorite candidate" and urging her "Pee Wee Marine" to be "the best Marine the Corps has ever had . . . enjoy it."

That seemed to be his plan. By late October, it might be argued that Steve "Football Head" Joyner had sailed through the course. "He looked like a linebacker or a Marine officer," said fellow candidate John Powell. "He seemed to ooze confidence and had very strong leadership abilities."

At Field Day competition two days before graduation, Joyner's platoon had lost so many candidates through attrition that it could not compete in all events. The platoon staff tried to use the personnel shortage to advantage by asking organizers if one of their candidates could compete in more than one event. The Field Day authorities approved, as long as the candidate in question did not have the last name "Joyner."

Capt. Stensland's OCS platoon, October 1966 (Joyner, 4th row, 4th from left).

Five

THE BASIC SCHOOL

On 28 October 1966 at Quantico, Steve Joyner graduated from OCS as a second lieutenant in the U.S. Marine Corps Reserve. Although his family could not attend the ceremony, a close friend from the La Habra High football program did.

Lt. Joyner had invited former co-captain and good friend Pat Moretta—now an Army private stationed at nearby Fort Belvoir—to attend the public commissioning ceremony. Afterward, Moretta drove Steve to the Marine Corps Officer Basic School (TBS) at Camp Barrett, located within the Quantico base about eight miles from OCS. While Joyner checked in at TBS, Moretta walked around the headquarters building. Because Pvt. Moretta's Army uniform had large brass engineer's insignia on the collar, many freshly minted Marine lieutenants from a distance mistook the shiny metal for a major's bars, saluting as they approached him.

An embarrassed Moretta attempted to be the first to salute, but the lieutenants seemed to beat him to the punch each time. A Marine sergeant major almost did the same. At the last moment, however, he recognized the uniform, put his hand down, and muttered "damn Army" as he passed.

———

The Basic School 3-67 (the third class in Fiscal Year 1967) welcomed more than 500 new lieutenants. The overall purpose of the course sought to build on the skills introduced at OCS. Tactical small-unit infantry leadership—a focal point of the training—emphasized the role of an effective infantry platoon commander to lead with confidence. The course was also designed to instill pride in the legacy of a Marine officer, teach military virtue and bearing, and develop esprit de corps.

As TBS 3-67 began training in November 1966, there was an underlying and obvious urgency throughout the Corps for battle-ready junior officers . . . the war in Vietnam.

From 900 military advisors in the late 1950s, U.S. military involvement in Vietnam had escalated to 385,000 troops by the end of 1966. Although the majority of the American public still supported the war effort, casualties were mounting at an alarming rate—from 216 killed in 1964 to 6,350 just two years later.

Marine Corps combat units entered the conflict in March 1965, trained, as always, to be prepared for any contingency. By early 1966, Marine Corps recruitment of officer candidates on college campuses reached full-throttle.

A strong sense of patriotism pervaded the outlook of all TBS 3-67 lieutenants. They wanted to serve and welcomed the prospect of receiving orders to Vietnam. That's why they joined the Marine Corps.

Many Basic School lieutenants were sons of World War II veterans. They accepted the government's Cold War goal of containment of the Soviet Union and China, and the "domino theory" that we had to stop communism in Vietnam or risk the fall of all Southeast Asia and beyond. Better to fight the communists in Vietnam than to fight them at home.

The lieutenants of TBS 3-67 believed that preserving the freedom of the non-communist Republic of South Vietnam was a just cause. Victory was an attainable—and necessary—goal over the North Vietnamese communist aggressors.

Most lieutenants, however, lacked an understanding of the political developments in the Vietnam conflict dating from French colonial rule. Neither did they know the extent of the corruption in the South Vietnamese government. They were unaware of the magnitude and growing support in the south for reunification with North Vietnam.

The compressed Basic School training schedule allowed little time to teach candidates about the recent history of Vietnam and how the United States became engaged in the war. Lieutenants left TBS with a modicum of knowledge of Vietnam's history and a limited insight of its cultural context. No fault of the well-meaning, hard-pressed TBS instructors, but lieutenants received little insight into the evolution of the tactical combat history in the I Corps area of operations of Vietnam, where they would serve. These lessons had to be learned the hard way—upon arrival in the field.

As expected, training was rigorous with the dangers ahead never downplayed. For many lieutenants, especially those from states with moderate weather, the winter of 1966-1967 came as an unpleasant shock with freezing temperatures that included a full dose of snow, ice, rain, and wind. Whatever the conditions, field training continued as scheduled.

Outdoor activities included military skills and tactical infantry training—map reading, weapons demonstrations and familiarization, rifle and pistol qualifications, and other evaluated skills. During tactical exercises, lieutenants were assigned various student billets and graded. Of course, superior physical conditioning played an integral part—the obstacle course, runs and hikes with full gear, endurance exercises, marching, and more running.

Joyner attacking the obstacle course

The indoor classroom often proved a respite. Adjoining the Basic School headquarters, the instructional building included four large, multi-tiered classrooms with long rows of tables. An important element of TBS was that each major academic course of instruction included tests during the training cycle. Ultimately, the academic segment of training comprised about 25 percent of the TBS evaluation.

Given the fast pace of instruction, candidates had limited time to study the material before testing. Study halls helped some officers, but on the whole a lieutenant either absorbed the material or he didn't. Some officers struggled, including Joyner, whose academic average hovered near 70 percent.

Furthermore, field training schedules provided little time for sleep, making staying awake and alert difficult during classroom sessions. Instructors often used unorthodox techniques to keep exhausted lieutenants engaged. Some walked on student tables during their presentations to emphasize a teaching point or, more often, to keep lieutenants awake. Other instructors resorted to gimmicks, using bawdy jokes and colorful language. Some made dramatic statements to grab attention before a substantive presentation.

Most instructors offered well-prepared lectures on relevant subjects that lieutenants could use upon arrival in Vietnam. An effective and motivated presenter might have a fair chance of keeping attention. A marginal instructor, however, could prove deadly. Dated training films shown in warm, darkened classrooms ensured that a few lieutenants would nod off.

Instructors told lieutenants if they had trouble keeping awake during the presentations they should stand up and go to the rear of the classroom. Most students avoided that for fear of attracting unwanted attention from the staff and out of concern of peer derision. Thus, they often tried to doze while sitting up. Some excelled at catnaps. However, a few sleeping students would inevitably fall out of their chairs, to their personal humiliation and the delight of most everyone else.

———————

The packed five-and-one-half days per week training schedule left little time for getting to know TBS classmates. Daily social contact was usually limited to suite mates, those rooming in close proximity, and those with whom they dined in the cavernous O'Bannon Hall Bachelor Officer's Quarters (BOQ) mess hall. On weekends, lieutenants who resided at the BOQ drove to main side Quantico or clustered around the few televisions at O'Bannon to watch college and pro football. Sunday brunch allowed them some latitude on when to take their meal, but the young officers often spent what remained of their weekend preparing for the training week ahead.

The Basic School class was further divided between married and single officers. Married lieutenants lived off base, but stowed uniforms and training gear in the BOQ room of two bachelors. For the most part, they also socialized in off-duty hours with other married officers, further limiting opportunities to know colleagues on a personal basis.

A number of single lieutenants sometimes partied hard on weekdays as well as weekends. Some of those even found time during the workweek to drive to Georgetown bars, the all-female Mary Washington College in Fredericksburg, or other locales where female companionship could be found. Driving off base for extracurricular activities in the evening made it difficult but not impossible for adventurous lieutenants to make early morning formation in the required uniform and training gear.

Joyner corresponded with and, on occasion, dated various women over the course of the Basic School program, having little trouble locating attractive ladies. Thanksgiving and Christmas holidays allowed lieutenants a few days to travel home or to meet with their girlfriends. After his relationship with Bev subsided, Steve saw a photo of Anne, a cousin of family friends in Pennsylvania, and asked to be introduced.

Steve and Anne, 1967

Joyner's physical fitness at the Basic School equaled his prowess at OCS. He occasionally traveled 20 miles to Georgetown with platoon classmate Sam Kelly to enjoy the weekend social scene. At one party, with their dates watching, Joyner astonished the group by going to a door column and, without effort, pumping out 15 one-armed pull-ups.

Kelly considered Steve to be his best friend at TBS. "One of the greatest guys I ever met," he said. "His sister made shirts for him. If I were in combat, I would want him watching my back."

Steve also enjoyed spending time with his roommate, John Keepnews. They were an interesting contrast in appearance—the 6'1", 210-pound Joyner with the 5'8", 155-pound Keepnews.

Lt. Joyner was at ease with other lieutenants, always approachable. "You could let your guard down with him," said Joe Gerry, a friend since San Diego State who would become a cardiologist after being wounded in Vietnam. "He was not defensive, but an instant friend."

Joyner supported the purpose of training for war at TBS, even if his performance in some areas, such as the classroom, might have fallen short of his goals. Capt. Jerry Paull, a former enlisted Marine and Virginia Military Institute graduate, commanded Joyner's 46-man TBS platoon, Fox Company Second Platoon. Paull noted that Joyner extended a helping hand to other lieutenants in an evaluative training environment that many Basic School officers viewed as a hyper-competitive, dog-eat-dog world.

The intensity of constant competitive pressure and close quarters could easily lead to bickering among the classmates.

Basic School lieutenants were sometimes quick to criticize or even belittle peers who they felt fell short of their self-imposed standards.

When fellow officers held assigned student billets such as platoon commander or squad leader, Joyner always cooperated with them and followed their orders without question. In part, perhaps because Steve encouraged fellow classmates and avoided judging others, lieutenants trusted and confided in him.

Lt. Joyner fit the common stereotype of a Marine officer. "A man of action, a hard charger," said Capt. Paull.

Instructors and classmates appeared universally touched by his thoughtful Christian demeanor. As always, they viewed him as outgoing, enthusiastic, and fun. He may have looked like a California beach boy turned all-American football player, but Steve was always a team player.

"He had it all," said platoon classmate Jim Hughey. "Size, attitude, acumen, calm, control . . . a cheerleader who led from the front, a Marine's Marine. He appeared proud to be a Marine, prouder than his peers."

Moreover, TBS classmates pointed out that Steve's character traits appeared to make him a natural leader whose troops would admire and respect once he found his way to the field in Vietnam. There seemed little doubt that Lt. Joyner would ask more from his platoon than he did of himself, that he would be the perfect infantry officer to lead young Marines in Vietnam.

As noted, TBS prepared all 544 newly commissioned lieu-tenants of Class 3-67 to be basic infantry officers. The program also offered exposure to an array of functional jobs available to a Marine officer. Several weeks before completion of TBS, lieutenants identified a preferred Military Occupational Specialty (MOS) and two alternate choices. Assignment to a MOS depended on preference and class standing, but the most important factor was the needs of the Marine Corps in Vietnam at that particular time. More than 60 percent of the TBS class were assigned to a MOS other than infantry, delaying their ar-rival in Vietnam by several weeks or months.

Lt. Joyner also had the option of playing football for the Quantico Marines. With a tradition dating back to 1919 and an annual roster filled with former college football players, the Quantico Devil Dogs would compile nine undefeated seasons against all-Marine, inter-service, and collegiate opponents. Following the lead of other military bases, Quantico would ter-minate its football program in 1972.

But, by 1967, Steve had already ended his football career. He never seriously considered playing football for the Quantico team. He wanted to lead men in combat. His choices for a Military Occupational Specialty were 1) infantry, 2) amphibi-ous tractors, and 3) artillery. Despite his modest class ranking, Joyner's higher than average military skills and conditioning scores in part encouraged his company commander to rec-ommend him for the infantry "with confidence." Perhaps even more important was Joyner's stated reason for wanting the infantry MOS: "I joined the Marine Corps to protect the lives of American men and women. I feel I can best fulfill that goal by leading a Marine rifle platoon."

In early March 1967, the final month of TBS training, Joyner had just completed the intensive "Three Day War" in freezing temperatures. During preparation for a scheduled amphibious landing exercise near Little Creek, Virginia, he received his next assignment. In what must have been somewhat of a surprise, if not disappointment, he did not receive orders for Vietnam. Instead, he would report to Camp Lejeune, North Carolina with the Second Division before an expected follow-up assignment to Vietnam.

On 29 March 1967, after five months of intensive training, 544 lieutenants graduated from The Basic School. Joyner landed in the 53 percent not immediately going to Vietnam, those assigned either to schools for additional training or non-Vietnam duty stations. Nine percent headed to Pensacola for flight training and 38 percent were assigned without delay to Vietnam, most as infantry officers.

Forty-seven of the 41st Officer Candidate Course and TBS 3-67classes would fall in combat. That included 11 Marine Air Wing officers killed in action as pilots or navigators. The rest were ground officers. In addition, two 41st OCS staff non-commissioned officers would die in Vietnam. One of them, Staff Sergeant Karl Taylor, would posthumously be awarded the Medal of Honor.

Steve's roommate at TBS, John Keepnews, would die in combat near Khe Sanh on 7 June 1968. It is not known whether Lt. Joyner received the news.

TBS 3-67, Platoon F-2, March 1967 (Joyner rear row, 5th from right)

Six

GUANTANAMO BAY NAVAL STATION

Following graduation from TBS on 29 March, Steve flew to Los Angeles for two weeks of home leave before reporting to Third Battalion, Sixth Marines (3/6) at Camp Lejeune, North Carolina. Now commanding an infantry platoon of 46 Marines, Joyner described his outstanding quarters to his sister. "I have my own 'house' with maid service and all," he told Kaaren. "Boy, I never expected this."

After a month of preparation in North Carolina, the battalion of about 800 men—four companies of Marines, four platoons per company—boarded a Navy ship in early May and sailed to the U.S. Naval Station at Guantanamo, Cuba (GTMO) for a four-month tour as a Ground Defense Force on the island. Several of the lieutenants had been together at

Quantico. John Keepnews, Steve's old roommate, also commanded a platoon in 3/6, as did Norman Lane and several other TBS classmates.

At GTMO, as the heat and humidity soared, the battalion undertook intensive training in preparation for possible assignment to Southeast Asia. "The training," he wrote, "is entirely counter-guerrilla in nature: search and clear, destroy, patrolling, population control."

Even so, the Lieutenant had told his family that his next assignment might be the Mediterranean. By all indications, that would have been a disappointment to him. He had trained and been geared for combat duty in Vietnam.

At Joyner's request, the 3/6 battalion commander appointed him lay leader, a position that required high moral character, motivation, and religious interest. Active in his ascribed faith, a lay leader could lead religious services in the absence of a chaplain while deployed. For those Marines who were devout, a lay leader could definitely boost morale.

Lt. Joyner also had duties as education officer, mess officer, and junior officer during courts-martial proceedings. He wrote his sister that the first two trials ended with the accused "put into the base brig for one month and reduced to the next pay grade."

While the letter to his sister began with a request that she send him some homemade chocolate chip cookies, preferably wrapped "in a sports section of a newspaper," it concluded

Guantanamo Bay, May 1967

with a conundrum that would follow Lt. Joyner throughout his service—how would he lead and support his Marines while answering to a superior officer who might have other priorities?

"My job here in GTMO has been one of many decisions and responsibility," he wrote. "Possibly the most important is the welfare of my men. I am responsible for every action (pro or con) and must stand up for them to our company commander. I like every minute of this work, for these men look up to you and respect you for your duties and work. I only pray to God that He continues to guide me and give me strength."

It is possible, if not likely, that the lieutenant had experienced a misunderstanding or difference of opinion with his company commander. While he might have been conflicted whether to choose his platoon or his commanding officer (CO), he appears to have decided to support his Marines. This choice would be repeated in Vietnam.

Still, there remained little doubt that he relished his job and the responsibilities as platoon commander. He seemed focused on building morale. "I'm running with the platoon each day after working hours to keep them in shape," he wrote, "and this builds that team spirit!"

Lt. Joyner (center) and his platoon at Guantanamo, May 1967

He mentioned that his platoon had requalified at the rifle range and that he had worked hard to prepare them for a CO's inspection. "My job has kept me very busy these past few weeks. July 26th was Independence Day for Cuba, so our battalion commander put us on 'special alert.' We are still in this status."

To enhance his academic training, Steve completed several Marine Corps Institute correspondence courses, including Tactics of the Marine Rifle Platoon and Map Reading.

Four months at Guantanamo did not include all work. During off hours, the officers often played volleyball. In mid-August, Lt. Joyner spent five days of R&R in Puerto Rico.

By September 1967, the battalion wound down training at Guantanamo and began to plan for the return to Camp Lejeune.

With assignment to the Mediterranean no longer in the forecast, Joyner received orders that upon completion of duty with the Sixth Marines, he would have a month's leave before reporting for duty in Vietnam with the Third Division.

———

Performance evaluations of Joyner's initial professional experience in the Fleet Marine Force seemed both tough and positive. His battalion CO noted, opaquely, that the young lieutenant was hard working and dedicated, having "begun to grasp the essentials of a Marine officer and that he had made considerable progress in recognizing the most serious responsibilities of a platoon commander." Describing him as "outgoing and affable," his reporting senior noted that the lieutenant epitomized the image of a Marine officer and led by example. While the CO gave Lt. Joyner top marks in cooperation and personal relations, he marked him down in judgment and initiative, not all that surprising or unusual for a new lieutenant just out of The Basic School.

An evaluation written months later by the same commander noted Joyner's progress, recognizing "his growth potential in the areas of command and personal leadership are substantial. As a staff officer it is probably somewhat limited."

In his correspondence with family, the lieutenant made no mention of his evaluations, and there is no indication in his records that he read or had been informed of the details of his officer fitness reports.

Upon returning to Camp Lejeune in September, Steve called his mother, admitting that "hearing her voice made him feel like he was home again." A few days later, he would write that he looked forward "with all my heart" to seeing everyone in October. Like most in the military, he had his bouts with being homesick.

Seven

CALIFORNIA

In late September 1967, Steve left North Carolina in his small VW, bound for home leave in California. His good friend John Keepnews left Camp Lejeune at the same time to visit his new wife in New York State. The two lieutenants planned to re-unite in California for a couple days before boarding the military charter aircraft that would carry them to South Vietnam. Keepnews had not seen the west coast and Joyner wanted to show him the sun and shore.

Steve first spent time with his mother, younger sister, and extended family in La Habra. In mid-October, he drove to San Diego to bid further farewells.

He had hoped to catch a San Diego State football game, but the schedule did not cooperate. The Aztecs were the nation's number one small college team, in the midst of a 25-game win streak. In fact, Coach Coryell's team had not lost since Steve's senior year. The Aztecs had outgrown the stadium in the heart of the campus to play before sellout crowds at the 48,000-seat San Diego Stadium. Coryell's recruitment of numerous JC prospects had already changed the face of the team. Steve knew few of the players.

Joyner surprised and delighted Coach Coryell with his visit. They talked football, of course, during a warm and lengthy meeting. But Coryell—who had been an Army paratrooper during World War II before playing football at the University of Washington—mostly wanted to hear about Steve's Marine experiences and what he expected in Vietnam. Again, Coryell mentioned that a coaching position awaited once Steve had fulfilled his military obligation.

While the lieutenant did not refuse—he was too respectful and gracious for that—football had been completely replaced on his radar by the Marine Corps and Vietnam. The gridiron now behind him, the road ahead beckoned, harboring unknown challenges that Joyner appeared eager to experience.

Joyner also visited the Sigma Phi Epsilon house to say goodbye to his fraternity brothers. Opposition to the Vietnam conflict had grown on campuses throughout the country in the 16 months since Steve's graduation. The social discord included a festering conflict within the fraternity over the war that would last for several years, members taking opposing viewpoints with emotions raw and sometimes quite vocal.

Even so, a great deal of excitement surrounded Steve's visit. At an afternoon gathering in the chapter room, attentive fraternity brothers listened as an animated Joyner described the details of his Marine training. He appeared fit, sharp, and his stories transfixed those present. Beyond explaining his motivation for wanting to serve in Vietnam, he spoke about the tactics a Marine rifle platoon would use to take an enemy objective. He told the group that he was prepared for whatever he might encounter in Vietnam. He had received the training needed to succeed and looked forward to leading Marines in combat.

During ensuing questions and discussion, silence prevailed as Steve mentioned the mortality rate of second lieutenants. Like the others, Hil Contreras could not help but ponder for a moment whether his friend might not return alive from Vietnam. The more he listened, however, the more convinced he became that Steve would return unscathed. Lt. Joyner's training, his confidence and determination, and his concern for others, Contreras concluded, would help ensure his safety and that of the Marines under his command.

Not surprising, Joyner was respectful to fraternity brothers who might not share his viewpoint. Fraternity president Bob Gaines, who had opposed the war since its outset, had a private talk with Steve next to the fraternity swimming pool. Each friend listened courteously as the other described his view of the conflict. Although exchanging polar arguments, there was never any tension or anger.

"It was a very passionate and upbeat discussion," said Gaines, "filled with smiles and understanding. We agreed that we both wanted what was best for America. Steve stressed, however, that it wasn't the war he loved, but his sense of patriotic duty that propelled him to Vietnam. 'And don't worry, God has my back,' he told me emphatically."

Gaines explained that all the fraternity brothers—despite the sharp disagreements about the war—respected Steve's conviction.

"Steve believed wholeheartedly in what he was doing and would not be deterred from pursuing his goals," said Gaines. "He also had this sense of physical strength and readiness . . . that he had never been in greater shape in his life and the Marine Corps had given him the ability to handle any situation."

A similar picture of Joyner's enthusiasm for his assignment to Vietnam emerged when he headed north to Napa, where his sister Kaaren taught school. Several days before departure, he drove around San Francisco with childhood neighbor and friend Tani Salant. As with his fraternity brothers, Stephen noted how Marine Corps training had provided him the best possible preparation for Vietnam. He explained to Salant that his training gave him the skills he needed to survive his combat assignment. At the time, his conviction calmed her concerns.

During the visit with Kaaren, Stephen seemed upbeat, even joyful. She taped him talking and singing. When he left, quiet and utter sadness descended upon her.

The date initially scheduled for departure, 10 November 1967, marked the 192nd birthday of the Marine Corps. It would take four days—including a stopover in Okinawa—to fly from Northern California's Travis Air Force Base to South Vietnam. Joyner made the journey with two friends from TBS and Guantanamo—John Keepnews and Norman Lane. Like so many heading to war for the first time, all three Lieutenants would certainly have had a lot on their minds—faith, excitement, anxiety. After more than a year of training and preparation, the time had arrived. Would they measure up to the job? Could they lead their men and keep them safe? Steve Joyner felt prepared, but the test would come when he stepped in front of his platoon.

Before boarding the plane for Vietnam, he mailed a brief note to his mother:

Dearest Mom,
　I can't really put on this paper how my heart feels at this time . . . I love you with all my heart and always will.
　God keep you until we are together again.

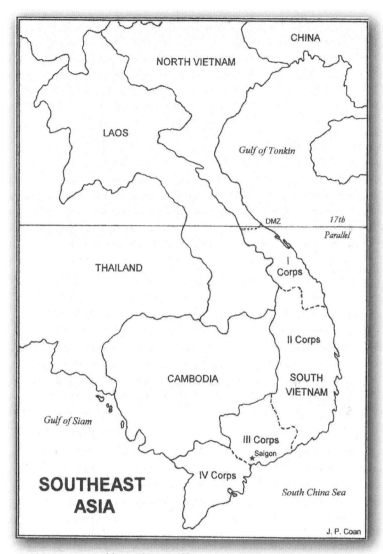

Lt. Joyner would spend most of his tour in Vietnam near the DMZ
(with permission, James P. Coan, *Con Thien: The Hill of Angels*)

Eight

LIMA COMPANY

On 20 November 1967, Second Lieutenant Joyner joined Lima Company of the Third Battalion Fourth Marine Regiment (3/4). The 3d Battalion command post was located just south of the Demilitarized Zone in the northern-most sector of South Vietnam, approximately 14 miles east of the South China Sea and two miles south of the besieged combat base at Con Thien.

Joyner had already viewed much of the terrain—known as Leatherneck Square—that the Third Marine Division was attempting to protect from the invading North Vietnamese Army (NVA). Approximately six miles wide and nine miles deep, Leatherneck Square included Marine Corps combat bases at each corner—Con Thien, Firebase Gio Linh, Dong Ha, and Cam Lo. From the time Marines had moved into the area in March 1967, the 54-square miles of jungle and hills had been the stage for intense fighting with the NVA.

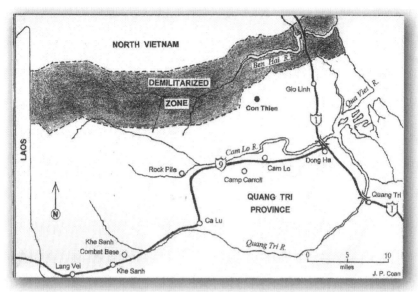

DMZ Area Marine Bases in I Corps (1967-68). The borders of Leatherneck
Square connected Con Thien, Gio Linh, Cam Lo, and Dong Ha.
(With permission, James P. Coan, *Con Thien: The Hill of Angels*)

Joyner, Lane, and Keepnews had initially flown from Okinawa
to the Third Marine headquarters, located on the southeast corner of Leatherneck Square at Da Hong. Based on officer needs of
the moment, Joyner and Lane were assigned to 3/4, Keepnews
to the Second Battalion Ninth Marine Regiment.

Transported by helicopter to the northeast sector, Joyner
was sent directly south to the Cam Lo Bridge (C-3 Bridge) where
his new company held position. Two days later, Lima moved
back north to defend the C-2 Bridge, called The Washout.

The Lima company commander gave Lt. Joyner the Second
Platoon, consisting of 43 Marines, two Navy Corpsmen, and
one Vietnamese scout who had once been a Viet Cong. "This is

what I wanted," he wrote home to his mother, "to be in this uniform with these men."

Fellow lieutenant Ken Christy, who had been in the company a couple months, observed that both Joyner and Lane expressed enthusiasm over the prospect of getting to the field, to spend as much time as possible gaining experience in the "bush." Lane would soon be sent to H&S Company.

On 1 December, Joyner was promoted to first lieutenant, from brown bar to silver. Lt. Jim Day, the former Second Platoon commander who had been promoted to Lima Company Executive Officer (XO) upon Joyner's arrival, noted that the newcomer seemed "really squared away" and looked forward to leading his men in combat. "He was a big bruiser, solid muscle," said Day.

When Lt. Day turned the platoon over to Joyner, he urged that Steve listen to his veteran platoon sergeant, James Ables, and "keep his mouth shut" until he got his feet on the ground.

In establishing his style of command, Joyner paid attention and listened to all of his Marines, making an effort not to steal the show and not to act without regard to how his troops might be impacted. He quickly learned the names of all his men, tried to establish personal ties with them, allowed anyone to talk at troop meetings, and worked to make a tight platoon. He respected his men and they respected him.

"He could be stern but was soft spoken, not a screamer," said Day. "And he was always smiling . . . a genuine half grin with a good sense of humor."

That personality would be quickly tested in Steve's relationship with his direct superior and commanding officer. "My company commander, Captain Carr, is very military in his attitude and actions," he wrote his mother. "He keeps after us lieutenants like nobody's business."

Days later, Joyner expressed worry in a letter that he might have trouble meeting the high expectations of a Korean War-era Marine who gave no quarter to his lieutenants, personally holding them responsible for the actions of their platoon members. "At times I feel I just can't do the job my commanding officer wants me to," he wrote to his mother, "for he is a hard man to understand. Each day, it seems, I have to account for some event my Marines have been involved in. I must be honest and straightforward in each decision when explaining to the CO what might have happened. May God help me in the coming months."

Joyner found Capt. John Carr to be a demanding and difficult, if not impossible, taskmaster, as did all the lieutenants in Lima Company. Sarcastic, perhaps well-meaning but often demeaning in his treatment of subordinate officers, Capt. Carr came down hard on every Lima Company lieutenant, Joyner included. Carr viewed all his lieutenants as inexperienced and deficient by definition. In his view, they required his constant, critical guidance. A tough and courageous officer himself, Carr doubtless believed that close supervision was the key to keeping his Marines alive. Two months before Joyner's arrival, Carr had

lost eight Marines—including two lieutenants—in an accidental drowning incident during a flood at Cam Lo Bridge.

"That had to be a major factor in the way Carr functioned
after losing so many to non-combat fatalities," said Lt. Day, who
had arrived at Lima a few days after the tragedy. "That was probably the main reason he was so hard on his junior officers."

Like other reserve lieutenants in Lima Company, Joyner was
on the receiving end of the wrath of a regular, career officer
who countenanced no missteps by his platoon commanders.
Although Steve never alluded to any bias against reserve officers
in his company or battalion in letters back home, many lieutenants in Vietnam experienced it first-hand.

Within weeks of joining Lima Company, a dejected Joyner
spoke confidentially to XO Day. Looking for guidance to his
dilemma with the commanding officer, Steve expressed frus-
tration that there seemed little he could do to please Carr.
Day urged Joyner not to worry, assuring him that Carr equally
distributed his contempt among subordinates. Day added that
he was chewed out by the captain nearly every day. Even so,
Joyner's platoon sergeant, James Ables, thought that Capt.
Carr for some reason appeared especially tough on the young
lieutenant.

A TBS classmate familiar with Steve's difficulties thought the
explanation was obvious. His COs disliked the rapport the lieutenant easily established with his Marines and were envious of
an effective leadership style that seemed so out of step with the
hard core approach they were taught as junior officers.

In any event, Steve's early encounters with Capt. Carr seemed to have affected his self-confidence as a platoon leader. Steady, negative feedback from the company commander must have left him with the feeling that perhaps the most important senior officer in his chain of command did not value his judgment or have his back.

Beyond his enlisted Marines and commanding officer, Joyner also had to earn the respect of the other lieutenants in Lima Company. Again, most of his infantry officer classmates at The Basic School had gone directly to Vietnam. Lt. Joyner's assignment to Camp Lejeune and Guantanamo delayed his arrival by six months. This complicated professional and personal relationships with officers who might be junior in rank, but senior in field experience. Even lieutenants who had graduated from officer training after Joyner had already proven their abilities in the field by the time he arrived in the battalion. Lt. Day, for one, had graduated TBS two classes after Steve, but was senior in rank due to his prior enlisted experience.

Sgt. Ables, a 12-year career Marine with seven months in Vietnam, immediately took Joyner under his wing. "Please don't worry," Steve wrote to his mother, "for I have the best platoon to look after and they really look after me in the field, especially Sgt. Ables."

While he respected the NVA, Lt. Joyner assured his mother that victory was inevitable. "I know the Marines will bring the war to an end and peace to the Vietnamese."

Steve's main complaint seemed to be the wet and increasingly cold weather: "It has yet to clear up or stop raining since my arrival. This situation will continue until late January. I just can't get used to so much rain."

At the same time, he tried to downplay to his mother the intensity of combat: "Right now, there is not a great deal of action. We set into squad-size ambushes during the night and do receive sniper fire, but not heavy artillery."

In fact, enemy activity during most of December seemed more of a harassing nature around 3/4's area of operations south of Con Thien—daily sniping at patrols and Marine combat positions, intelligence gathering, and observation of Marine activity. That lull did not equate to less danger.

"I really know what people mean when they say the lieutenants make their money in Vietnam when the action starts to hit," Joyner wrote. "For I must expose myself and make sure my units are supporting one another and that our fire is delivered on the target."

Third Battalion activity included company and platoon-level operations, as well as small-unit patrols, called Hunter-Killer teams. A more effective intelligence gathering tactic than moving larger units through the countryside, the patrols extended up to 4,000 meters (2.5 miles) from base to report on or engage small enemy reconnaissance and infiltrating units. The patrols consisted of six to nine Marines, to include an officer, two snipers, a corpsman, radioman, and at least one rifleman. A reinforced squad with machine guns could run 12-15 Marines.

With potential danger lurking everywhere around them, they cautiously navigated small rolling hills and rice paddies bordered by dense underbrush. "I really work, both mentally and physically," Joyner wrote. "My biggest job is to maintain the troops during firing. We often receive sniper fire on our patrols and coordination between squads must remain."

From the outset, Lt. Joyner put everything he had been taught at Basic School into effect. He slept little, never showing fatigue to his platoon, although he must have felt it. He tried to ensure all the details of his job were properly handled. He strived to be the best officer he could be and wanted in return to win the respect of his men. Aside from providing tactical leadership in field operations, the lieutenant inspected weapons daily. He checked his platoon's chow, mail, and living conditions, functions that could have been done or shared more fully by his platoon sergeant and squad leaders.

———

While relatively more secure than the surrounding countryside, combat bases were not viewed as safe havens. Every Marine base near the DMZ lay within range of enemy artillery and mortar fire.

"The last two nights we have been hit with small arms fire— automatic weapons and mortars," Joyner wrote. "The company commander called in Arty (artillery) and then an air strike on their withdrawal route."

Lima Company rotated patrol duties among each of its three infantry platoons, augmented by the mortar and machine gun sections of the company weapons platoon. When not in the field, a platoon would stand watch on the base perimeter, hardening their defensive positions by filling sandbags and digging deeper fighting holes.

———

The early weeks of command could be perilous for an inexperienced platoon commander. While showing senior officers and peers his competence, he had to demonstrate to his enlisted Marines the ability to command, convincing them that he had their best interests at heart and would not do anything rash that would place them at undue risk or danger.

Additionally, the learning curve for every Marine could often be rapid, the demands of war swiftly turning rookies into veterans. Despite having the private doubts and fears that every combat Marine in Vietnam experienced, Lt. Joyner demonstrated more than his share of confidence. But, to maintain control of a platoon in a combat environment, he also needed to understand the importance of relying on his more experienced senior enlisted Marines to keep him out of trouble as he found his footing in the field.

To reiterate, Lt. Day had suggested Joyner pay close attention to the suggestions of his platoon sergeant. To Steve's benefit, James Ables had a reputation for being one of the best and most competent staff noncommissioned officers (NCOs) in the battalion. He had the know-how in the field and had earned the confidence of the 3d platoon's enlisted Marines, the company commander, as well as the regard of other NCOs.

Misunderstandings or a struggle for control between a junior officer new to the field and an experienced platoon sergeant were sure recipes for creating major tensions and control problems within the platoon.

Respecting his senior enlisted man's expertise with added praise for all of his NCOs, Joyner relied on Ables for advice when he assumed command. At some point, however, he apparently told his platoon sergeant that he, the lieutenant, had ultimate responsibility for the platoon's activities. It might have been a minor incident, something that Lt. Joyner and Sgt. Ables would soon get over. The issue to Steve, however, was one of principle.

"My platoon sergeant has been great up until now and it is up to me to continue to impress upon him the importance of our job and his position in the chain of command," wrote Joyner. "Every once in a while I have to get after my three sergeant squad leaders for telling the troops some 'bullshit' or something. This is not the place to tell 'sea stories' with the troops."

Joyner's leadership style—straight out of The Basic School playbook—contrasted with that of his predecessor. Lt. Day, who had enlisted in the Marine Corps before he was selected for officer training, believed that a platoon commander had to rely on his subordinates to get things done. Joyner's impulse seemed to want to rely less on his NCOs. Unlike Joyner, Day held few platoon formations. He relied on Sgt. Ables almost exclusively to run the platoon. He issued orders to Ables, who in turn supervised the squad leaders and platoon guide (responsible for logistics) in working out the details of the day's activities. Day believed that this approach of pushing accountability down the chain of command empowered the platoon sergeant and squad leaders to exercise and develop small-unit leadership.

In contrast, Joyner followed the doctrine that the lieutenant alone was in charge of his platoon and, therefore, the responsible Marine. In 1966-67, when Joyner went through training, TBS instruction on leadership at the platoon command level did not emphasize the critical importance of NCOs and the potential pitfalls faced by a junior officer platoon commander leading more experienced enlisted Marines in Vietnam. The training focused on the all-knowing, all-responsible lieutenant who retained firm control of his platoon. Lieutenants were taught to never blame more senior officers for unpopular orders they had to carry out. Like Day, Joyner always took full responsibility for any order that he gave.

"I must do what the Marine Corps has taught me to do," he wrote.

To his credit, Ables claimed little difficulty adjusting to Joyner's leadership style. He advised the lieutenant when appropriate, but would step aside and accept Lt. Joyner's final decision. While they had their occasional disagreements, both remained friendly and respectful of one another.

Naturally, Steve had little problem creating personal bonds within his platoon. He was not a self-absorbed officer. He experienced disappointments, like every other officer, but aside from his early relationship with Capt. Carr, brushed them off with relative ease.

Projecting energy and enthusiasm, the hard-working lieutenant genuinely cared for the welfare of each man. In turn, his men respected and admired him.

———

But did they feel comfortable following him in war? It was a critical question and one that every officer in Vietnam faced with trepidation. Until a new lieutenant successfully led his platoon through tough spots fraught with danger, his Marines had a "show me" attitude. Enlisted Marines expected officers to prove their competence in the field—the ability to exercise good judgment, make the right decisions, and demonstrate "street smarts." To their mind, a platoon leader had to possess the self-confidence that he would protect the unit and, whenever possible, avoid unnecessary risks that could cost lives, even if that meant sometimes questioning the judgment of more senior leaders. While assigned missions and objectives were important, in an increasingly unpopular war with diminishing support on the home front, enlisted Marines in infantry units expected officers to place their safety and welfare before all else.

It didn't matter that Lt. Joyner had the look of a perfect Marine or that he pushed his troops as hard as he pushed himself. His fighting spirit, high energy, and let's-get-it-done decisions were not always appreciated within the ranks and seemed at times to conflict with their expectations. Even his leadership qualities might have been questioned. According to one of Joyner's Second Platoon squad leaders:

> He would volunteer us for nearly every dangerous mission that came up. When we had returned from being in the bush for many days at a time, he seldom gave us needed time off or a chance to rest. He would immediately volunteer us for a patrol or night ambush. Lt. Joyner was in great shape and had lots of energy, but most of his troops had been in Vietnam quite a while and we were battle weary. As a result, many became bitter since they thought he was trying to make a name for himself at our expense and was bucking for a promotion. I even resented his actions at times. It took time however for me to realize that in his mind, he thought he was doing what was best for the Corps. He was a brave Marine.

Incessant patrolling, along with sweep and destroy operations, sapped energy from already exhausted, tense Marines. As a lieutenant who most often took directions from his senior officers without hesitation, it would have been in perfect character for Joyner, according to Day, to at times volunteer his platoon for assignments without understanding how it might cause their alienation.

"At present we patrol daily," Joyner wrote home at one point, not mentioning that he might have had his platoon working harder than they wanted. In truth, all infantry units in-country were continually stretched to the maximum work load and sometimes beyond that, often worn down to the point of exhaustion from little sleep, few opportunities to keep clean, and the strain of constant combat activity.

Still, Joyner might have been unaware that some Marines interpreted his gung-ho approach as that of a self-serving junior officer. He now found himself in the crucible of combat, working in an environment altogether different from any he had experienced before. Elements of his character that football coaches and friends admired in civilian life—empathy for others, affability, cheerfulness, unquestioned obedience to authority, and unbridled enthusiasm for the job at hand—were not always valued by battle-hardened Marines who counted the days remaining on their tour in "Nam." Above all, they wanted to return to "the world."

C ontemporary judgments of Lt. Joyner are not at all in agree-
ment. Yes, his Marines recalled his consistent concern for
their welfare and his efforts to connect with them as individuals.
In an environment where many officers intentionally tried to
keep a distance from their Marines to insulate themselves emotionally from the possibility of losing them in combat, Joyner
took the opposite tact. At the risk of overstatement, he perhaps
regarded his Marines almost as teammates, much like his fellow
football players at San Diego State.

Nevertheless, some thought such familiarity inappropriate
and felt that he appeared too close to his Marines. A 3/4 Marine
who did not serve directly under Joyner heard from several in
his platoon that the lieutenant did not demand enough of them.
He appeared to them a personable "frat guy," more a buddy with
his subordinates than a leader.

Lt. Joyner had several other attributes that his troops began
to note. On occasion, he seemed reluctant to share information, perhaps concluding that his Marines did not always need to
know the big picture. He appeared to think that simply issuing
an order was sufficient, a characteristic that some in his platoon
did not appreciate.

He also had an occasional quirk of interrupting his own dis-
course while making a decision. Sometimes, in mid-sentence,
he would back off a train of thought, rephrase his narrative,
and reach a course of action different from his original plan.
Some Marines viewed that as a lack of confidence on Joyner's
part. Several fitness reports from his commanding officers,

including two before Vietnam, made reference to Joyner's questionable judgment.

Perhaps unknown to Lt. Joyner, six weeks after his arrival, Capt. Carr submitted a fitness report on the lieutenant that would be approved and signed by the battalion commander. The assessment was consistent with what one might expect from a lieutenant new to Vietnam, reflecting Joyner's inexperience and his efforts to adjust to a difficult combat environment. Joyner's initial performance appraisal in Vietnam noted that while he was a "congenial, enthusiastic officer, his lack of self-confidence impeded him in dealing quickly and effectively in new situations," and that he required "detailed supervision in his handling of subordinates." Still, Carr thought Joyner "showed promise of developing into a fine troop leader and Marine officer."

Meanwhile, like most officers, Joyner strived to convince others that he was decisive and in complete control, despite any personal worries that he might not measure up to the standards expected of him. Although, over time, Lt. Joyner grew in confidence, Lt. Day wondered if the early difficulties he encountered as a platoon commander might have carried over for the rest of his tour in Vietnam.

———◆———

Adding to the complexity of being a new platoon commander was dealing with the growing disillusionment with the war itself. U.S. troops in Vietnam followed developments back home through Armed Forces Vietnam radio broadcasts, *Stars and Stripes* newspaper articles, and letters from home. By November 1967, the press and public opinion in the U.S. had begun to turn against the war.

"It was a time when we heard all the turmoil and war protests going on back home," said one Marine who served under Joyner later in the lieutenant's tour. "We all felt like we had no business being there and wondered why we were sacrificing our lives for an unappreciative country. Even most of the people we were fighting for and trying to protect resented our presence. It was demoralizing."

Marines continued to win the battles, but with mounting casualties, morale and discipline grew more tenuous. Platoon commanders, especially those with limited experience in Vietnam, could not always expect blind obedience to orders. That made sound troop handling more difficult and more important. It also further subjected the decisions made by junior officers to more scrutiny by their Marines.

Respect for and adherence to authority figures certainly worked for Steve in football programs from his teens through college. It seemed to be the template he brought to Marine Corps training and it was reinforced at Basic School. But in a combat situation, Lt. Joyner might not have fully understood that orders from an officer did not always translate into unquestioned obedience.

Nine

NEW GUY MISTAKES

In most ways an exemplary Marine officer, Lt. Joyner would nonetheless experience a few early bruises to the perception of his leadership. Every junior officer shared the experience. Some recovered from them, others had a more difficult time.

The night before an assigned patrol, Sgt. Ables had stayed up late talking with a Marine buddy from another battalion whose unit had passed through the area. During the evening, Ables instructed Sgt. James Rebar, responsible for the platoon's logistics requirements, to be sure he was up in time for the scheduled patrol. The next morning, when Rebar told Joyner he had to wake Ables, the lieutenant told Rebar to let him sleep. The lieutenant thought he was doing Ables a favor by giving him a much needed break.

Sgt. James Ables and Sgt. James Rebar

While on patrol, the platoon came upon a pile of U.S. bomb debris. An excited Joyner, perhaps anxious to exert his authority in the platoon and eager to win the respect of the company commander, reported by radio to Capt. Carr that his platoon had found what appeared to be remnants of an enemy rocket launcher.

When one NCO tried to convince Joyner that the debris was not an enemy rocket launcher, Joyner insisted he knew what U.S. ordnance looked like. According to an eyewitness, Joyner pulled rank, reminding the Marine that he, Joyner, was the platoon commander. As the platoon returned to base with multiple bomb fragments in the pockets of a number of Marines, Ables met them at the gate, unhappy that he had been left behind to sleep.

At the same time, Capt. Carr, waiting with battalion commander Lt. Col. Bendell, asked to see the enemy rocket launcher fragments. A grinning and proud Joyner presented the officers with the debris. After looking at what Lt. Joyner had brought back, a disappointed Bendell said nothing and left. Embarrassed and furious, Capt. Carr first took Ables aside and asked how he could have let the incident happen. Carr then admonished Joyner within earshot of Ables and other nearby Marines, calling him "stupid" and ordering the lieutenant to "get that shit out of this compound."

Returning to the platoon area, a dejected Joyner said to Ables, "Go ahead and say it Sarge . . . say I fucked up."

This incident must have proven a bitter learning experience; both a setback to winning the loyalty of his platoon and the confidence of his superiors.

In another December incident, Capt Carr radioed the lieutenant during a patrol, asking for his platoon's location. Rather than use secure check-points as reference, Joyner gave the platoon's location in actual grid coordinates in the clear. Upon hearing the exchange on his radio, Sgt. Ables jumped up and immediately directed the squad leaders to take their Marines out of the area. About five minutes later enemy mortars impacted where the platoon had just left. Lt. Joyner did not realize that the enemy might be monitoring the radio transmissions.

Leading his platoon on another routine patrol, Joyner radioed for an artillery mission on an enemy target, but the incoming rounds detonated dangerously close to his men. The lieutenant had not known the exact location of his platoon.

———

Those three incidents might be defined as common "new guy" mistakes similar to those made by countless other lieutenants, hardly the entire picture of Joyner's efforts and impact. To be fair, many of his actions earned the praise of senior officers.

In early December, during an operation to an area where food, weapons, and ammunition had previously been stored, Joyner's patrol captured three enemy troops and their weapons. They faced a "small" firefight on the way back to base, but were unable to advance toward the enemy due to terrain features.

Later in the month, Joyner's patrol got involved in a heavier skirmish. Safely back at the base, he wrote home, proudly noting the positive comment he had received from Capt. Carr:

Hello from the land of popup targets! Today I really had a time on the patrol. Leaving at 0630 first light, we started out for an objective which yesterday air strikes had six confirmed North Vietnamese Army regulars killed. When my patrol approached the objective area we "locked-on" with an NVA unit. Only our fire power and fire control gave us the victory. We had one WIA, a chest wound. He was medevaced and on the operating table in about 12 minutes! The enemy took a loss of seven KIAs. I was quite proud of my unit today, as always, and the skipper gave me a "job well done." Numerous weapons and food supplies were also taken by my patrol. Tomorrow is another day . . . I contacted the hospital and received word from the doctor that my Marine was in fine condition and will go to Japan for six weeks to recover.

Despite the continuous peril and the reported deaths of several TBS classmates in the weeks following his arrival in Vietnam, Joyner remained positive with the letters he sent home. While he tired of the weather, "very cool with rain, both heavy and light, 24 hours per day," at least he had been issued wool long johns to help thwart the wetness and temperatures now dipping below 40 degrees. Plus, he was maintaining his strength. "The chow is really good," he wrote. "We have at present (and why I say this is that it is subject to change at a moment's notice) two hot meals per day morning and dinner. For lunch, that's right, C-rats!"

He asked his sister for a dark green sweatshirt to blend in with the terrain and told his mother that there were a number of California flags at camp, wondering if she might ask the Elks to send him one. "I would be very proud and appreciative of the gift."

Steve washing clothes at C-2 Combat Base

He expressed gratitude for care packages sent by friends and relatives, particularly the soap, canned goods, and writing paper sent to him by the La Habra Firebelles—the women's auxilliary to the fire department. In a heartfelt thank-you note to the Firebelles, he gave them a sense of a Marine's life in Vietnam and a brief look into his value system:

It is our mission to conduct offensive, multi-company operations. We patrol daily with squad-size ambushes at night. There are no Viet Cong this far north in South Vietnam. We have daily contact with the NVA, who are highly trained in tactics and small arms weapons. They only fight when they have you under their conditions or else you have them cornered and they must fight. They are experts in camouflage and withdrawal of their dead and wounded . . . I love my job, family, country, and God.

Lt. Joyner let the folks back home know that he greatly respected the Vietnamese, adding that some of the elderly men reminded him of his grandfather. When sunshine finally made a three-hour appearance, he was ecstatic. "The sun really does shine in Vietnam."

Joyner could even joke about the accommodations, fondly recalling the luxurious bachelor quarters back at Camp Lejeune. "This foxhole, along with my radioman, really doesn't give me a helluva lot of room. It sure couldn't be labeled a BOQ."

As Christmas approached, hot meals had been reduced to one a day. But that didn't seem as difficult as the wave of homesickness experienced throughout the battalion. The lieutenant's family formed his bedrock of emotional support. "Say, I haven't even told you yet how much I love you and miss your sweet smile," Joyner wrote his mother. "You know I think of you continually and pray that God will watch over you until my return. At this time of year, we often think of the wonderful blessings we have, and the biggest one I will always have is your love and understanding."

The 24-year-old lieutenant also included a poem he had written to "fully express my thoughts about being apart from you this Christmas and the endless love I have for you."

> Even though we're far apart
> When Christmas time comes due,
> Warmest wishes cross the miles
> With special thoughts of you . . .
> Wishes for your happiness,
> For health and joy and cheer
> And all that makes your Christmas
> A merry one this year.

"I pray next year," he wrote to both his mother and sister, "we will share the best Christmas of all, togetherness."

December 25, 1967 – From left: Capt. John Carr, Lt. Col. Lee Bendell, Lt. Joyner, Lt. Jim Day, Lt. Tom Hoare, Lt. Ken Christy

On Christmas Day 1967, at the Washout, a photo was taken of all the officers of Lima Company with the battalion commander Lt. Col. Bendell. Weeks later, first platoon commander, Lt. Tom Hoare, would be killed in action. Capt. Carr and Lt. Ken Christy would both be seriously wounded in action and medevaced.

Ten

EARLY 1968

Joyner's platoon remained at the Washout until 27 December. It then moved north with elements of the battalion near The Trace—a strip of cleared jungle and undergrowth just south of the DMZ measuring 11 kilometers long by 600 meters wide. The northern border of Leatherneck Square, the Trace connected Con Thien on the west and Gio Linh to the east.

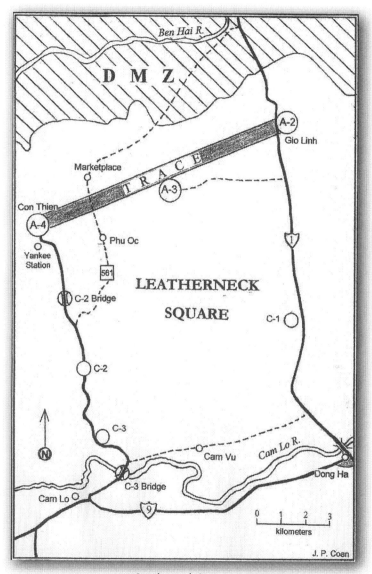

Leatherneck Square
(With permission, James P. Coan, *Con Thien: The Hill of Angels*)

The strategic purpose of 3/4's move was to provide security during the construction of a station to house radar equipment. The base at A-3 had become a key piece of the Strong Point Obstacle System, the ill-fated McNamara Line scheduled to be completed in the spring of 1968 for detection of enemy movement into South Vietnam.

———————

The pace of the war across northern Quang Tri Province took a sharp turn for the worse as the old year gave way to the new. An estimated nine NVA regiments—consisting of 21,000 combatants—operated just south of the DMZ. Captured enemy documents suggested an impending major communist offensive throughout the country, probably at the end of January or early February during Tet, a traditional time of celebration for the Vietnamese New Year. On several occasions in late December and early January, U.S. aerial observers reported large numbers of NVA troops moving in the open.

Moving closer to the DMZ unsettled the Marines of the 3d Battalion, not just because of the added exposure to the NVA forces in the area, but that they would be replacing three Marine battalions.

As action picked up, many Marines, Joyner included, felt a sense of foreboding and uncertainty over the course of the war. For everyone, it was getting tougher to be away from home.

On New Year's Eve, Steve penned a brief note to Kaaren: "As I sit here in my foxhole, I can see the DMZ 400 meters to my direct front. The contact (with the NVA) has been increasing since our arrival. With God's help, I will return in one piece."

He thanked her for sending him a green sweatshirt to ward off the cold. "I haven't taken off the sweatshirt since its arrival," he wrote. "It keeps me warm and dry."

On 3 January, Platoon Commander Joyner again wrote his sister, sketching out what a normal daily schedule in a base area might be: "0600 – Up, shave, chow; 0700 – Morning report to CO w/ammo count and injury list; 0900 – Inspection of weapons; 1100 – Possible class on care in the field for the Marine & his weapon; 1200 – Tactics class; 1300 – Chow; 1330 – DTA (Daytime Activity, patrol, platoon-sized); 1700 – Return & report to CO's meeting with patrol report; 1900 – Start night watch and set out NTA (Nighttime Activity); 2200 – Check positions and squad watchers; 2400 – ?? – Hit the rack! (Read letters, look at pictures, think heavy, etc.)"

Platoon commanders were also assigned on rotation for additional duties. Lt. Joyner had just returned as pay officer, completing a helicopter journey from the "bush" to the division headquarters at Dong Ha to draw $9,000 to pay the troops. Unfortunately, Joyner came out $3 short, which he would personally cover. "It sounds easy," he told Kareen, "but by the time you go all over the country to pay our company personnel, you have a four-day job ahead of you."

On 4 January, he had time to write his mother, noting that Capt. Carr had given him another "job well done" as pay officer. He again mentioned the 38-degree weather, the nonstop rain, the near impossibility of keeping warm and dry. Hot meals were now to down to zero. "The chow is now Cs three times a day, which plays funny things on my excretion system (you know what I mean)!"

Worse, of course, was the tactical situation. "After the No Fire on New Year's, contact has increased," he wrote. "We have had contact on each patrol since the holidays."

He could not ignore the melancholy yearning to be home. "I love and miss you more than I could ever express myself on this small piece of paper," he closed. "Please do not ever forget that, Mother. I must close for now and inspect weapons and (defensive) positions, for dark is only an hour away."

During the first week of January 1968, Lt. Joyner had become the Lima Company executive officer. While he would fill in for platoon commanders when there was a need, his regular duties would be more administrative in nature—tending to service record books, inspection of rear elements (office personnel), awards, pay records, equipment, processing Lima KIAs and investigations. One immediate investigation to which he was assigned involved a Marine in Lima Company who had intentionally shot himself in the foot to avoid further combat.

Lt. Joyner enjoyed working with the battalion XO and appeared pleased with his new responsibilities, which he seemed to have thought were a better fit for him than leading a platoon in the field. "The hours are longer, if that is possible," he wrote Kaaren, "yet I feel the responsibility gives me more confidence."

Lt. Joyner also viewed his promotion to XO as opening future career prospects. He seemed to be thinking of perhaps making the Marine Corps a career. "I can now work toward that staff or company commander job upon my return to the States," he wrote. "The new office for me holds a lot of challenges and opportunities."

Capt. Carr thought Joyner's accomplishments as XO were admirable. "The myriad of administrative duties inherent in the executive officer job was tackled with enthusiasm, vigor, and determination," the commanding officer would later write. "The many investigations he was assigned were accomplished after many hours of tireless research and roadwork on his part. Lt. Joyner always put forth with a maximum effort in all that he did."

Even Lt. Day noticed that Joyner, after becoming XO, had apparently won the confidence of Capt. Carr.

Dan Moore

While engaged in almost continuous combat with NVA regulars, the Third Battalion would be involved in three major, costly battles during January. During the first half of the month, the battalion would remain north of combat base A-3, near Hill 28 and the village of An Phu. On 7 January, Lima fought a battle with NVA troops approximately 2.5 miles northeast of Con Thien, just above The Trace. The company lost four Marines and 16 had to be medevaced. At least 33 NVA were killed.

In that encounter, Joyner and machine gunner Mike Talley took turns carrying wounded Marines on their backs from the battlefield. Talley stated that he would have gone anywhere to fight under Joyner's command. Capt. Carr later wrote that he witnessed XO Joyner and his reserve platoon carrying numerous Marine casualties over 2,000 meters [1.25 miles] of rough terrain to the Marine casualty point on the base perimeter.

On 12 January, most of the battalion's units moved just south of The Trace to patrol the An Dinh-Phu Oc village areas near the abandoned Marketplace. It was dotted with rolling hills broken by thick hedgerows and open grassy areas containing numerous NVA fortified bunkers and trenches.

The Marketplace became the scene of a second, more intensive battle on 18 January. Just a mile east of Con Thien, Lima Company faced off with a company of the 803d NVA regiment armed with mortars, rocket-propelled grenades (RPGs) and artillery support. The 16-hour encounter cost the battalion 11 killed and 33 wounded. Lt. Hoare, 1st platoon commander, was killed in an ambush at the outset of the battle. Capt. Carr was seriously wounded while extricating wounded Marines surrounded by the enemy, for which he earned the Silver Star. During the medevac—which could only proceed after U.S. air strikes and artillery fire—Carr was fortunate to survive when his helicopter took enemy fire. The Marines killed nearly 200 NVA.

The horror of the 18 January clash wore heavy on all of the Marines, Joyner included. As XO, he immediately visited wounded Marines on the *USS Repose* off the coast. "They will be aboard the ship for some time due to injuries," he wrote Kaaren two days after the battle.

Steve also asked his sister not to tell their mother what he had recently experienced. "I must say, it was as close as I have ever come to death," he wrote. "I hope and pray I will never come that close again . . . I never want to remember the sights and events I have encountered, so I will never take pictures of this time in my life." In fact, Lt. Joyner took not one known photo during his tour in Vietnam.

Despite being shaken by the recent battles with the NVA, Lt. Joyner's commitment to what he was doing did not waver. "I believe in this job," he wrote. "I will defend it with my life."

Writing to his mother several days later, he did not mention the increase in hostilities. Instead, he focused on her financial situation. Still mourning the death of her husband, June had decided to cut expenses by selling the family home in La Habra and moving into an apartment in Fullerton. Without a job, she had been living on a monthly allotment of $100 transferred from her son's paycheck that would increase to $275 beginning 1 February. At the same time, with her son's assistance, June had successfully applied for status as a dependent with the Marine Corps, adding an additional $50 each month.

———

E nemy activity in Leatherneck Square and elsewhere in I Corps continued to escalate. On 24 January, elements of a fresh NVA regiment ambushed a small convoy and a subsequent relief force on Route 9, northwest of the major Marine artillery base at Camp Carroll. In response, Marine helicopters transported troops to positions on and around a prominent hill straddling Route 9. Intelligence suggested the NVA might be trying to close down the road and assault Camp Carroll.

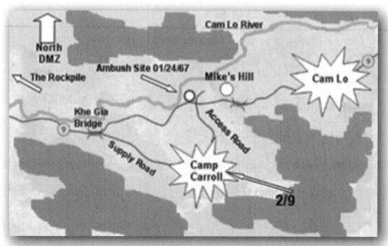

Mike's Hill, Route 9, and Camp Carroll

Lima Company, with XO Joyner and the new commanding officer, Capt. Larry McLaughlin, arrived on 25 January at Mike's Hill. Named for Mike Company of the Third Battalion, the high ground overlooked and straddled Highway 9 from the north. That evening, the battalion deployed into its initial three-company defensive perimeter around the base of the hill.

By morning 26 January, the enemy had completely encircled the battalion on Mike's Hill. Firefights raged throughout the day. In the early hours of 27 January, the enemy began a full-fledged assault to overrun 3/4. But the NVA found the perimeter had been moved, under darkness, higher up on the hill, making them easy targets for the entrenched Marines. Waves of attacks resulted in hundreds of NVA casualties, but at the cost of 21 Marine lives and 62 WIA.

After the Marines beat back the assault, General Westmoreland congratulated the officers and men of 3d Battalion for holding Mike's Hill and preempting an enemy attack against Camp Carroll.

Over the course of heavy fighting in January, the battalion had inflicted significant losses on the enemy. In this grinding war of attrition, the 3d Battalion had lost three officers, six corpsmen, and 39 enlisted Marines.

In late January, enemy forces began to encircle Khe Sanh. The NVA had closed Marine road transport to Khe Sanh the previous summer, but Route 9 from Dong Ha to Ca Lu remained open, linking division headquarters at Dong Ha with Marine combat bases, including Camp Carroll and the Rockpile.

As Tet approached, Marine Intelligence expected heavy ground and mortar attacks throughout I Corps. In western Quang Tri Province, the enemy's siege of Khe Sanh continued to tighten. The base came under daily NVA artillery fire and NVA forces shut down transport on Route 9, requiring all supplies and troop reinforcements by air.

Despite intelligence suggesting an imminent communist offensive, U.S. and South Vietnamese forces were surprised at the scale of coordinated attacks that began at the start of Tet on January 30. The February Tet Offensive throughout Vietnam included Saigon, Hue, district and provincial capitals, and major U.S. and Republic of Vietnam military bases. With the exception of Hue, where the battle lasted 26 days, communist forces were beaten back and suffered crippling losses within days of the offensive.

While the First Marine Division took the brunt of the attacks in southern I Corps during the Tet Offensive, Quang Tri Province near the DMZ was comparatively quiet. The NVA had little reason to press an isolated and over-stretched 3d Division that could provide limited assistance to embattled towns and cities under NVA attack in provinces to the south. Third Marines withstood isolated attacks at district headquarters and easily repulsed an assault at Quang Tri Provincial headquarters.

After several days at Camp Carroll, Joyner spent most of February with elements of Lima Company providing road security at Ca Lu base, west of Camp Carroll along Highway 9. During this time, he was informed that he had been selected to fill a battalion quota to attend a one-month embarkation course in Okinawa during March.

By the end of February, Lima Company had moved east to the Cam Lo District headquarters, near the vicinity where Joyner had arrived in Vietnam back in November. Although it lost two Marines KIA and 27 WIA, February had proven to be a relative respite for 3d Battalion as it recovered from the high personnel losses of January.

Eleven

OKINAWA

The March '68 Embarkation School at Okinawa's Camp Hansen featured a class of about 40 Marines who filled quotas from major commands in Vietnam. Attendees enjoyed a month of classroom instruction, after which the Marine Corps designated them embarkation-qualified.

Arriving in Okinawa on 4 March, Steve anticipated a much appreciated rest. "I will learn how to put a Marine battalion aboard a Navy ship," he wrote. "I think I will enjoy it . . . sure beats being shot at!"

His activities after class, he joked, would consist of "sleeping, working with weights, and writing letters."

For most students, the school became a de facto extended R&R. Classes ended each day at 5 p.m. With little to no homework, evenings were free and relaxed, the weekends open. Students had opportunity to socialize at the nearby Officer's Club with other lieutenants going to or leaving Vietnam. They had time to decompress, but on the downside, had ample time to ponder the day they would have to return to a combat zone.

While some did not expect to deal with embarkation matters for the rest of their tours, Joyner took a conscientious approach to the program.

———◆———

Although we had both attended The Basic School together, I did not know Steve Joyner until meeting him in the Embarkation School class. During the month-long course we would establish a close friendship, facilitated in large part by the relaxed, non-combat environment. Had we met in Vietnam, we would not have had the same opportunity to talk and reflect on what we had experienced and might face in the future.

We became fast friends and had conversations ranging from duties in war to our plans after Vietnam, with the confidence that discussions would be kept to ourselves. As I had recently spent five months with a line infantry company, what he had experienced in Lima Company resonated with me.

As we talked, I was impressed with his candor and honesty. Although I now know that he was troubled by what he already had been through, he did his best not to show it. He carried himself with a calm dignity. At that point in my life, I could never have had a more important friend.

I had arrived at Okinawa in shock and silent grief. Two weeks earlier, Lance Corporal Ken Stetson—my former assistant forward observer—had been killed in Hue during the Tet Offensive. My world, for the first time in Vietnam, had been turned upside down. Steve listened to my story about losing Stetson with quiet empathy.

LCpl Ken Stetson, January 1968

From the day I had arrived in Vietnam in August 1967, Stetson and I had worked together as forward observers in Golf Company, 2d Battalion 5th Marines, 1st Marine Division (2/5). A native of Longmont, Colorado, he joined the Marine Corps not long after high school graduation. Ken had married Jan, his high school sweetheart. Quiet, deferential, earnest—he had a slow, western drawl and a dry sense of humor. On our four-man forward observer (FO) team, Ken became my right-hand man. Although he had attended Artillery Forward Observer School in preparation for his assignment to Vietnam, over five months I taught him everything I could about being an FO. I depended on him.

In early 1968, I left Golf Company to fill in as a battalion fire support coordinator with the headquarters section of 2/5. Although another officer was unavailable to take my duties as FO, I did not worry. With LCpl. Stetson, I was leaving the care the company's artillery support in the best hands possible.

Stetson and Golf Company entered Hue on 31 January 1968, at the outset of the Tet offensive. In the battle for Hue, he fought with Golf as 2/5 gradually pushed the NVA south of the Perfume River—street by street—into the western suburbs of the city. Other elements of Fifth Marines and First Marines north of the river had their hands full in the fight for the old imperial city and the Citadel.

I entered Hue on 13 February with 2/5 rear, the battalion reserve from a company of 2/5, the battalion XO, and other headquarters sections. On the morning of 17 February, I had been calling in an artillery fire mission in support of Marines attacking NVA troops in the Hue Citadel. Following the mission, my jeep driver and I returned to the 2/5 headquarters compound in the abandoned Hue University faculty apartments. As I got out of the vehicle in the courtyard, I saw Stetson lying alone on a gurney about 20 feet away. In disbelief, I walked up to him and asked what had happened. Pale but lucid, he managed a weak smile and told me he had been shot. He pointed to a small bullet hole in his right upper abdominal area. He had been cleaned up and was not bleeding. In a weak but clear voice he told me, "Don't worry, Lieutenant, I'm going to be alright."

As I stood speechless, medical personnel loaded him in a vehicle that sped away to the closest helicopter landing pad. Taken to the hospital in Phu Bai, eight miles away, he died trying to dictate a letter to Jan. I have thought many times of that last meeting with Stetson. Seeing my own distress, he tried to console me. I only hope I provided some measure of comfort to him in return.

Delaying the awful task of writing Stetson's wife, I first wrote my parents:

Stetson is the big blond kid you see in some of the photos. I suppose I know him as well or better than anyone else here. We were together from the day I got to Vietnam until I left Golf Company. Stetson was a remarkable man – besides being an outstanding FO, he was the bulwark of Golf Company always doing things for people and never a complaint. I had quite a few close, personal talks with him. He was doing an infantryman's job when he was shot, leaning out of a window and firing at NVA. I can't help feeling a great loss over Stetson's death. Why do people like him have to die?

———

Amid the relative calm of Okinawa, I sat down to write Jan Stetson. I tried to explain what Ken had meant to me and why, mentioning his unselfishness and generous spirit . . . afraid that my words could not do justice to the deep respect I had for him.

I had lost a fellow Marine I regarded as a brother. But officers were not supposed to grieve. Officers were not supposed to cry. I was dealing with deep anguish but I had no one I could talk to about it until Steve Joyner appeared. He listened, offering words of solace, encouragement, and the importance of carrying on . . . of duty. Fully understanding how Stetson's death had affected me, he helped ease my sorrow. We both had to continue to march, he said.

In our talks, I also learned about Steve. He told me about his upbringing in California, being stationed in Guantanamo, and the season of experiences in Vietnam. His background as a college football star came out in time, but he clearly did not regard that as an integral part of who he was as a person or a Marine officer. He had moved on. Likewise, I did not view his football heroics as an important aspect of his character.

Although Steve revealed little about his personal views of the war and any misgivings he might have harbored, he speculated that, upon his return to Vietnam, he might be reassigned as a battalion staff officer. Infantry officers who survived four-to-six months in the field were often moved to a staff position at a battalion headquarters for the remainder of their tour. In most cases, a staff assignment carried marginally less risk of becoming a casualty than leading an infantry platoon. Joyner, however, had just over three months in the field when he left for Embarkation School. Even so, taking a battalion staff officer position to reduce his risk was not a goal—it simply was not what he was about.

While Steve always tried to project a positive demeanor in our talks, it sometimes appeared forced. I sensed an underlying disquiet. He often seemed deep in thought or concerned about something.

In one conversation, he expressed uncertainty about his post-Vietnam plans. While I told him that I planned to leave active duty after my three-year commitment, he appeared undecided. I thought then that he leaned toward leaving the Corps.

Pat Moretta, an Army sergeant stationed in Okinawa, got together several times with his old high school football teammate. Moretta saw changes in his good friend. Steve appeared more somber and serious than the comparatively carefree, self-confident lieutenant whom Pat had seen in late 1966 at Basic School.

Joyner and Moretta in BOQ room, Okinawa, March 1968

From their conversations, Steve left no doubt with Pat that he was bearing the heavy weight of leadership and responsibility. Steve's body language and remarks conveyed concern over what he had already seen in Vietnam and what he knew he would face when he returned. Above all, in discussions with Moretta, Steve indicated that he wanted to avoid making mistakes in combat that might cost Marines their lives. He gave no evidence of worry that he might not make it through his tour. He had absolutely no regret for joining the Marines. In fact, Steve would tell Pat that he wanted to make the Corps a career.

Despite those introspective moments, Steve retained his positive outlook and displayed an impressive curiosity about Okinawan life. On a Saturday in mid-March, Steve and I hired a taxi to Naha and took in the local sites. I had my camera and took photos of street scenes. As we walked down one crowded commercial street, Steve stopped and said, "Let's go in here." I followed him into a small shop that sold custom-made kimonos. He explained to the mom-and-pop owners that he wanted to be fitted for a kimono. As I stood and watched in amazement, without comment, he confidently chose a burgundy colored pattern from a bolt of cotton cloth. Managing to communicate through the language barrier, the shop owner and his bemused wife took the measurements. Steve paid and agreed to pick up the kimono the following week.

That evening, we ate at a local restaurant serving traditional Okinawan food. We had more than one too many beers. Before returning to the base, Steve suggested we visit a brothel. When we told the taxi driver what we were looking for, he knew just the place.

With Embarkation School nearly over, Steve wrote his grandfather, describing his month in Okinawa. He had done well in the classes, worked out daily, gotten his weight back up to 210 pounds, and cherished his glimpse into another culture.

"The Ryuku people are so interesting and polite," he wrote. "The island has a fine university, a history museum, beautiful parks and clean beaches. I have some outstanding pictures which I am looking forward to sharing with you upon my return to the States."

Steve mentioned that the 30-day experience had been extremely enjoyable, but had "gone by very fast."

———————

My month in Okinawa came at a critical political juncture back home. The February Tet Offensive had been a turning point in U.S. public support for the Vietnam War effort. Yes, we had beaten back communist forces throughout the country, but their strong show of force and coordination in attacks against major cities and bases came as a shock to many of us. My views of the war were changing. I now saw no end in sight.

Although I felt considerable guilt for being away from my fellow Marines in Vietnam, March had been a welcome interlude from the forceful strains of combat, leadership, violence, death.

———————

Steve and I prepared to return to South Vietnam, he to an area near Con Thein and I to my battery located south of Phu Bai on National Highway 1. While 50 miles separated our destinations, it may as well have been a thousand. We discussed perhaps meeting up for our R&R, although at the time I thought it unlikely I could justify it after a month in Okinawa. We agreed to keep in touch and that I would send him the photos from the trip to Naha once I had them developed.

Twelve

BACK TO VIETNAM

Lt. Joyner and I both returned to our parent units in Vietnam on 4 April 1968. In the early morning hours of the following day, as I sat in the fire direction center of my battery, Armed Forces Radio broadcast the horrible news . . . Dr. Martin Luther King had been assassinated. A puzzled and heart-wrenching silence descended on the Marines of all races who listened to the reports.

The Marines of Lima Company were experiencing the same shock and anger. What, we wondered across South Vietnam, was happening back home?

While Lt. Joyner was away in Okinawa, 3/4 had shifted from the Camp Carroll area on Highway 9 to familiar territory near the C-2 and C-3 combat bases in Leatherneck Square. Combat casualties in the Third Battalion—15 killed and 67 wounded—worsened an already existing shortage of combat Marines in critical billets. Norman Lane, a TBS-colleague who had traveled with Steve to Vietnam back in November, was one of the fallen . . . mortar fire at Cam Lo Hill on 29 March.

Hostile action had momentarily quieted down and the debilitating heat continued to climb, now averaging 92 degrees with high humidity.

———

Over time, Joyner had developed into a more efficient and effective XO. He seemed to have hit his stride in the months following his return to Lima from Okinawa. Now a seasoned lieutenant, Steve looked after the company logistical requirements, focused on boosting company morale, contributed to tactical decisions in the field, and often led a platoon in the field when needed. He seemed to be everywhere, anticipating problems and needs. He carried out directives of the company commander, Capt. McLaughlin, with a close eye on the details. He had learned to elicit the advice of senior staff NCOs and held them in high regard. When appropriate, he made command decisions and expected his directives to be implemented. Lt. Day regarded Joyner as the best XO in the battalion. In Day's assessment, Steve had become "Mr. Lima Company."

As the months passed, Lt. Joyner's basic nature remained unshaken. Day viewed what he called Joyner's "gentle manner" as having an overall positive impact on his Marines. His large frame and sometimes stern look could be imposing to those who did not know him. That image, however, was quickly dispelled by a generous smile that won widespread trust. He was known "to be there" when things happened, at a major battle when things went wrong. He often took the blame when they did, but took adversity in stride and pressed on. As always, he treated his Marines with respect.

As XO, Steve constantly worked to make everything better. "He did all within his power and physical capabilities to motivate his Marines and to make sure that Lima Company had chow and ammo," said Day. "I think that if there was a USMC Dictionary, under the entry 'Marine Lieutenant' you would find a picture of Stephen Joyner."

Lt. Joyner received plenty of mail from family, friends, organizations (the Friends Church and Elks), and girls he had dated. In a 6 April letter to sister Kaaren that he wrote from Cam Lo Bridge, he made the surprise comment that when he returned home, he contemplated marriage, perhaps to Anne, the girl he had met when he was at TBS.

He also mentioned their mother, her move to the new apartment and the increased allotment. "I hope she is able to afford her medical equipment with this," he wrote. "I sure would like her to get a job."

Stephen closed with a birthday poem for Kaaren on the nature of love from 1 Corinthians 13:4-8 and the hope that they would share many more special days together.

Lt. Joyner wrote a letter on 17 April to a young Girl Scout in Southern California who had sent him a box of edible treats he had graciously shared with his men.

> Laurie Johnson—Many thanks from the Marines of Lima Company, 3d Battalion 4th Marines, 3d Marine Division. I am Lt. Joyner, XO of the company, who received a package from project Care. The package contained your name with your address on it. I want to express my warm feelings through this small note. I have passed the entire contents of the package throughout the company.

He closed with a short paragraph about himself and that he planned "to return home in early December, just in time for Christmas."

One of Joyner's XO tasks during that period involved an investigation into the circumstances surrounding the death of a 10-year old Vietnamese boy and injuries to several other children in a trash dump just outside C-2 base. The incident caused great anguish throughout the battalion.

Joyner, quite disturbed by the boy's death, had to determine any liability by the Lima Company Marines who had stood guard at the dump. Among the evidence Joyner had to consider was that local villagers would routinely sift through the garbage despite knowing the area was off limits and that at least one Marine—who had previously been admonished for allowing villagers into the dump—had thrown a white phosphorous smoke grenade into the area to scare away foragers.

Joyner's investigation, with some formatting input from Lt. Day, concluded that the guard who threw the grenade did not intend to injure the Vietnamese children and should be exonerated. He also determined that no negative repercussions would impact the Marine Corps. In fact, the Marine Corps—as was typical in such situations—provided the deceased child's family with a cash payment.

According to Lt. Day, if Joyner had concluded that the Marines on guard at the dump intended to harm or kill the children, he would have recommended punishment. No doubt this would have generated a problem for battalion leadership. Although he also agonized over the child's death, Lt. Col. Bendell would have likely been prepared to dismiss the incident as a regrettable misfortune that occurred in the fog of war.

April casualties had been comparatively light in the battalion, one killed and 13 wounded. The lull in combat would soon change, however, with the battalion's shift to Hill 689, a key combat base in defense of Khe Sanh.

On 19 April, 3/4 began the move to Hill 689, located near a major infiltration point for NVA forces moving south along the Ho Chi Minh trail. Hill 689 overlooked the Khe Sanh combat base about five kilometers (three miles) to the northeast and about the same distance from the Laotian border to the west. Hill 881N and 881S were to the north and Lang Vei U.S. Army Special Forces Camp to the southwest.

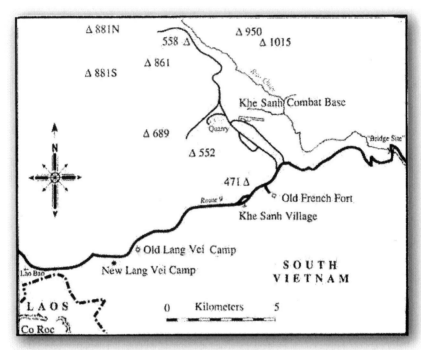

Khe Sanh and Adjacent Hilltop Bases
(With Permission, Michael Archer, *A Patch of Ground: Khe Sanh Remembered*)

Although U.S. forces in Operation Pegasus had broken the NVA siege of Khe Sanh and reopened Route 9 earlier in April, plans were underway to abandon Khe Sanh at some point in the near future.

By 22 April, the battalion command post with three companies, including Lima, had dug into defensive positions around the summit of Hill 689 and neighboring hilltops (552 and 471). "You wouldn't believe the action here," wrote Steve. "First

Marine Air Wing is giving us direct support on all our missions. Artillery is always planned as part of any patrol."

Along with not knowing how long they would occupy the hill, the situation was hardly comfortable. "We live in very deep holes with lots of overhead," he wrote. "The terrain is steep hills with grass about 15 feet high. The NVA have bunkers in this grass and on the slopes of the hills. He reinforces and has 60 and 82mm mortars capability. He is well trained & equipped and knows his areas of operation. He can be beat!! And is being beaten!"

On 27 April, Lt. Col. Bourne replaced Lt. Col. Bendell as the commanding officer of 3/4. Weeks later, Bendell would sign fitness reports on battalion officers from January through April, including Lima Company performance evaluations drafted by Capt. McLaughlin. Lt. Joyner was described as, "a highly motivated Marine who with greater experience and maturity should realize fine potential."

———

At the beginning of May, the battalion was short seven infantry lieutenants, about a third of its required complement. It also had 108 critical personnel shortages at the non-commissioned officer level and 163 enlisted Marines, mostly riflemen.

In support of the defense of Khe Sanh Base, 3/4's occupation of Hills 689, 881 South, 471, and 552 continued through the month. Casualties increased under steady NVA pressure, including mortar and artillery attacks and periodic probes of the company's defensive lines. With oppressive 96-degree heat and humidity, Lima conducted daily patrols and set up nighttime listening posts and ambushes to prevent a large-scale NVA attack. Marine intelligence indicated the possible presence of Chinese advisors among the NVA regular units.

Steve spent most of his time on Hill 689, with occasional brief courier trips back to Dong Ha by helicopter to welcome new arrivals, oversee company administrative activities, and ensure the company received the resupplies it required.

Taking full advantage of the few moments he might find to write home, Steve informed Kaaren that he planned to take his week-long R&R in July or August. He deeply missed friends and family, his appetite had fallen off with the hot weather, and there were no short cuts in war.

"My duties are divided among the following," he stated. "Work on night activities (e.g., ambushes, LPs, etc), investigations, and keeping my head down!"

Lt. Martin Traiser, a newly arrived platoon commander, initiated a conversation with the XO while standing above ground at the entrance to Joyner's underground bunker on Hill 689. A smiling Joyner interrupted and reminded him he needed to take cover in the bunker or risk becoming a casualty of NVA incoming fire.

Lt. Martin Traiser

Anticipating Mother's Day, Steve managed to send his mother a card and brief note on 6 May mentioning that he was sitting in his "officer's bunker" with "one eye on close air support missions to our North and the other writing to you." He added that he had requested duty assignments for 1) MCRD San Diego, 2) sea duty, or 3) HQMC in Washington, DC. He closed by telling his mother that he should be home by 10 December and "Thanks for the *Playboy*!"

Meanwhile, the battalion engaged in lengthy and heavy contact while supporting a division operation away from Hill 689 near the Cua Viet River north of Dong Ha in eastern Quang Tri province.

On 8 May, Steve's mother sent him a letter full of news about friends and, perhaps aware of his interest in possible marriage upon returning home, asked that he let her know if he ever became serious enough with a girl that it might lead to marriage. Steve assured her that he would keep her informed about any wedding plans . . . "although I sure have developed a romance." But, amazingly, a month after telling his sister he would like to marry Anne, he asked his mother about an old girlfriend. "How is Jan? Boy, she sure sounds great in her letters. Maybe."

On 10 May, the lieutenant found a moment to write Kaaren before returning to Hill 689 by helicopter. While thanking her for sending bedsheets that he had requested, he made no mention of Anne or Jan. In his only comment on the presidential primary season underway back home, he asked Kaaren what she thought of the Robert Kennedy campaign.

15 May 1968 at Dong Ha (from left): SSgt. James Ables, Lt. Richard Sergo, SSgt. James Terrell, Lt. Steve Joyner

He also asked her to watch for an old friend: "Kaaren, in early or mid-June, Marine Staff Sgt. James Ables will be coming to the Marine Corps Recruit Depot in San Diego for duty. He was my platoon sergeant while serving in Vietnam. I gave him your address and told him you could give him a meal and show him and his wife around until he gets settled."

As for the war, "Don't worry, everything is fine. We are killing some NVA."

———

The anti-war movement back in the States alarmed many servicemen in Vietnam. Letters from home as well as the civilian and Armed Forces media all reported the doubts and growing unrest of the American public. Lt. Day, for one, observed that as the troops grew more aware of a decline in support for the war, their own morale eroded. Lt. Joyner also took notice . . . and it bothered him.

In mid-May, Joyner penned a moving letter to the Fullerton Elks, where he addressed his concerns about the rising sentiment on the home front against the war. In earlier letters to family and friends, he had not commented on the anti-war movement. But a recent *Stars and Stripes* newspaper story about opposition to the war on a college campus evoked an eloquent defense of patriotism by the lieutenant. His well-argued letter revealed that he had thought for some time about what he put down on paper.

"Patriotism," Steve charged, "is not a dirty word to a young Marine sitting in the mud near the Demilitarized Zone."

The articulate philosophical essay (entire letter in Appendix A), revealed a Marine with deep respect for duty to country. "We're proud of being called patriots. It labels us loyal defenders of our country and its ideals. It's a good thing to have this feeling. It helps you to hold your head up high. It makes your country beautiful and you can feel this beauty. It makes you a better citizen. And if you are a better citizen, your country has to be the ultimate beneficiary.

"Let's tell people about patriotism. They'll understand. They might even get to like the idea . . . all of them."

The letter would be printed in the *Fullerton News Tribune* on 27 May, one of Steve's aunts forwarding it to The White House. President Lyndon Johnson's assistant, Whitney Shoemaker, assured Elnora Kling that the President "shares your pride in Stephen's statement of patriotism and purpose. His words . . . give added meaning to the President's efforts towards the goals of freedom, peace, and security."

By the end of May, Lima Company faced a stark shortage of effective officer and senior enlisted leadership. When Capt. McLaughlin rotated back to the States on 24 May, Joyner became the acting CO. The only remaining officer was platoon commander Martin Traiser. About the same time, SSgt. Ables left for duty in San Diego, replaced by a platoon sergeant who would be widely disliked by the troops.

On 28 May 1968, Lt. Stephen Joyner submitted the paperwork required to be considered for augmentation as a career officer in the U.S. Marine Corps. Speaking privately to one of his Marines, Joyner said he planned to extend six months in Vietnam beyond his 13-month tour with a chance of making captain.

Two days later, a Lima Company reconnaissance squad from the first platoon confronted an estimated six NVA on Hill 758, about a mile northwest of Hill 689. That the enemy had a .50 caliber machinegun indicated that a larger NVA unit could be nearby. With several Marines wounded and one missing, the squad formed a 360-degree defensive perimeter. Meanwhile, the remainder of the first platoon left Hill 689 to support the patrol. After evacuation of the wounded, the relief force called in artillery and air support to silence the enemy force and returned to Hill 689 before nightfall. The missing Marine had not been located.

Hill 689, May 1968

The following day, Joyner led a platoon-sized combat patrol in search of Lima's MIA. Artillery and mortar preparation fires preceded the platoon's move into the area. Amazingly, the lieutenant and his platoon found the missing Marine alive.

As the patrol moved across the top of a ridgeline on the way back to Hill 689, Lt. Joyner and his radioman were attempting to get a better view of the terrain from the crest of the hill when they accidentally revealed themselves. NVA forces spotted them and immediately brought the platoon under mortar fire, resulting in several Marines being wounded.

Enraged over what he perceived as a mistake by the lieutenant that threatened the safety of the patrol, a squad leader screamed at and berated Joyner in the field with a number of Marines present. When the platoon returned to Hill 689, Corporal John Hudson went to the lieutenant's bunker to apologize for an outburst that clearly violated the chain of command. Joyner could have pressed charges for insubordination, had he chosen to do so. Instead, a calm Joyner told him not to worry. "You were right, we should have stayed down," said Joyner about risking the lives of his men by going to the crest of the hill.

In a separate account of the incident, Corporal J.R. Spindler credited Joyner for possibly saving his life and those of other Marines when the lieutenant directed that the platoon should return to Hill 689 by an alternative route to the one they took earlier, thereby avoiding a well-known path the NVA had previously hit with mortars. Spindler described Joyner that day as cool under fire, an officer admired by his troops, a good and gallant Marine.

A subsequent debriefing of the missing Marine revealed that he had intentionally hidden during the earlier firefight. He had heard an unfounded rumor that if a U.S. serviceman went missing in action for three days, he could return to the U.S.

During May, the battalion suffered 31 killed and 237 wounded out of an average strength of 1,020 men. Even with 136 replacements, the battalion had a shortage of eight officers and 33 senior enlisted personnel. The crippling loss of experience and leadership had to hamper the effectiveness of 3/4 on Hill 689 and in the harrowing month that would follow. Having already experienced more than its share of combat over the course of many months, little did they know what they were about to face.

Thirteen

June 1968

Entering June, Third Battalion Fourth Marines, with its four rifle companies, still held Hill 689 and nearby hilltops in the vicinity of the U.S. combat base at Khe Sanh. Both the intense heat and NVA mortar attacks continued to climb. Again, the short-handed Lima Company had only two lieutenants, Steve Joyner and Martin Traiser. Joyner now pulled triple duty—XO, platoon commander, and acting company commander.

"The weather is a very warm 106 degrees today with humidity around 93 percent," Steve wrote Kaaren on 6 June. "Our patrols have been shorter somewhat due to the heat."

With enemy incoming fire, food and water resupplies were concerns. Nourishment remained strictly C-rations along with "special food rations." The company at times found itself short of water when the helicopters couldn't get to their position due to incoming enemy mortars.

"At present I am acting CO," he continued. "The company commander (Capt. McLaughlin) has rotated and his relief has not yet arrived in country. The job has kept me on the go, more than I could ever explain on this paper. The experience is good for me, I think it has given me confidence, stamina, and physical courage."

He did not mention to his sister that the NVA had been pounding Hill 689 with 82mm mortar rounds, about 150 rounds throughout the day and night. With support from the artillery battery at Khe Sanh, Joyner had repeatedly called night defensive fires around his position to discourage any plans for an all-out NVA ground attack.

"Still no news when we will leave this Hill and the Khe Sanh area," he continued to his sister. "It is getting so one area is just like the rest, and it really doesn't matter where you are."

The stress and weariness of war never eased and the oppressive weather made it worse.

"Please understand my lack to write neatly," he closed, with nightfall descending. "I can hardly see the lines on this paper. I love and miss you very much. God be with us both."

The assassination of presidential candidate Robert Kennedy in Los Angeles on 6 June once again shocked overseas military personnel. Two months after the Martin Luther King assassination, it appeared that American society and its political system were in chaos. Even so, war took precedence for those in combat. While Steve must have been deeply disturbed, he was too busy keeping things together in Lima Company.

On 9 June, orders arrived of an unfolding operation south of Khe Sanh. The following day, the battalion vacated Hill 689 by helicopters, spending the evening near the Khe Sanh airstrip. With plans for the entire combat base to be evacuated at some point in the near future, it would be important to keep the NVA at bay.

Khe Sanh Airstrip, 10 June 1968

On 11 June, the Third Battalion began participation in Robin South, a multi-battalion operation southwest of Khe Sanh designed to locate and destroy any enemy forces in the vicinity of the Montagnard village of Lang Hole, along with their weapons and supply caches. An infiltration route from the Ho Chi Minh Trail for enemy troops and supplies, the known NVA stronghold lay about 11 kilometers (seven miles) southwest of Khe Sanh and about 10 kilometers (six miles) east of the Laotian border. Again, disrupting the NVA infrastructure with a search and destroy operation in the surrounding areas and intercepting enemy supply routes would keep NVA forces on the defensive and benefit a secure evacuation of Khe Sanh.

First to arrive by helicopter near Lang Hole, Kilo Company came under immediate fire. Unfortunately, the landing zone sat close to a large NVA bunker complex. Two Marines went down in tall elephant grass and could not be located. The remaining companies of the battalion followed Kilo.

"Word was passed that we had lost two guys right out of the chopper," said Private First Class Gary Maxwell, who had only been in Vietnam a few days. "My squad was sent to reinforce Marine elements that had gotten into a firefight, but while in route they called us back. The NVA had broken off contact."

Shortly after their arrival, Lima Company formed a security perimeter and dug into trenches with Maxwell's squad getting the call to man a listening post.

"I remember the squad leader practically pleading with Lt. Traiser not to send us out," said Maxwell. "I was newly arrived and didn't appreciate the danger, but everyone was scared shitless. I believe that was the night one of our listening posts got spooked having heard movement, and came running into the perimeter. Three of the Marines were hit by our own machine gun, but survived after medevac."

The following afternoon, 12 June, the battalion's companies were again airlifted by helicopters about four miles farther south over rugged mountain terrain from Lang Hole to an area near Phou Nhoi, a hilltop located in an area surrounded by Laotian territory on three sides. But in the process of the move, three U.S. 250-pound bombs were accidently dropped near Marine positions.

Cpl. John Hudson was a Lima platoon squad leader with two fire teams and an attached four-man M-60 machine gun team. When they landed, the exhaust from the CH-46 ignited a fire in the dry and razor-sharp elephant grass.

"My squad was fighting a grass fire with our entrenching tools and shirts," said Hudson, "when the bombs hit less than 100 meters away."

The accidental bombing resulted in one killed and 15 wounded. Still, numerous contacts with the NVA by various Marine platoon and company-size patrols were having success as the enemy withdrew after initial contact, leaving behind base camps and supply caches which the Marines destroyed.

By 13 June, as directed, all of 3/4's companies had dug in not far from Hill 658 near Phou Nhoi hamlet in a battalion perimeter. It would soon become treacherous. During the day, Marine F-4 aircraft had dropped napalm bombs on a nearby hill with Marines in the vicinity. Fire from the napalm run quickly spread and unexpectedly threatened Lt. Traiser's platoon, requiring some Marines to run through the fire for higher ground.

When the platoon reached the top of a hill, they saw the fire rapidly approaching. Several Marines ran away from the fire and had to be retrieved. Traiser radioed Lt. Joyner for a helicopter extraction and was told to stay put. Soon afterwards Joyner and Captain Steven Austin, the new company commander, arrived with the rest of the company and created a fire break that successfully stopped the spread near their position.

Napalm Fire Near Phou Nhoi, 13 June 1968

Gary Maxwell's platoon, after landing by helicopter on the wrong hill, also had to scramble. "Fire from the napalm strike plagued us continually," said Maxwell, "and we grounded our gear and broke out our entrenching tools to fight it. Wind was whipping up the fire, and the word was given to get your gear and get away . . . not everyone found their gear and (friendly ordnance) started cooking off, wounding several Marines.

"Things settled down finally and we moved to two more hills, digging in each time only to have someone say, 'Saddle up, we're moving out!' By the time we finally got dug in at the last place, Hill 658, we weren't digging too deep."

On 14 June, after the fortuitous arrival, the battalion's companies dug in on Phou Nhoi. Lt. Traiser boarded a helicopter for his scheduled one-week R &R, leaving Lt. Joyner and Capt. Austin as the only officers in Lima Company. While action settled down somewhat, the enemy was clearly in the area.

Phou Nhoi Hill, 14 June

Lt. Day sat with Lt. Joyner on the battalion perimeter observing a distant Marine aircraft strike on a hill in the vicinity of Hill 658. As always, Joyner carried only a pistol, believing that a Marine officer could not lead effectively carrying a rifle. When Day asked him how things were going, a preoccupied Joyner replied "Okay" and suggested a correction in the aircraft's bombing run. Then Joyner suddenly left to join his Marines, saying he had things to do.

By evening, the battalion had established a 360-degree perimeter on the top of Phou Nhoi manned by an estimated 600-700 Marines. The most likely avenue of approach for a possible NVA attack lay in the northwest sector of the lines occupied by Lima Company.

Facing northwest, Cpl. Hudson's squad dug in about 250 meters from Hill 703, overlooking a steep draw that ran down to a small stream. A heavily used footpath ran directly from the streambed to the top of Phou Nhoi hill. Tracks and droppings on the trail revealed that elephants had been used by the NVA to move heavy loads. "We dug in that evening in our usual open-top fire team-size fighting holes," wrote Hudson.

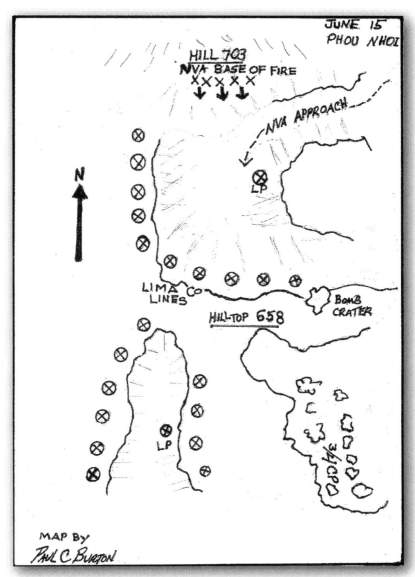

Map of Phou Nhoi Hill, 15 June 1968 (Drawn by Paul Burton)

In the dark at 0445 on 15 June, Lima Marines began to hear loud movement in the streambed at the base of Hill 703 to the northwest. "The NVA had made much noise all night long getting into position to attack," said LCpl J.R. Spindler, "without attempting to disguise their location or intent."

One hour later, the defensive lines of Lima Company received a barrage of rocket-propelled grenades (RPGs) and .50 caliber machine gun fire from Hill 703. The initial assault killed Marines dug in at a listening post in front of Lima's lines near the trail on Hill 658. One of those included LCpl Gerald Lavoie, who died without a visible scratch from a concussion caused by an RPG.

Lance Corporal Gerald Lavoie, spring 1968, killed at the battle of Phou Nhoi

Just before daybreak, the enemy followed with a massive ground attack by the reinforced NVA 4th Battalion 66th Regiment that overran several Lima Company fighting positions located on the lower, forward slope of Hill 658. NVA attackers had penetrated the perimeter. The battalion requested urgent support from Marine helicopter gunships and fixed wing aircraft.

"There was a lot of confusion and things were moving fast in an attempt to stop more NVA from coming inside," said Spindler. "We all had our hands full trying to keep from being totally overrun in addition to being mortared at the same time."

"Our people were mowing them down like grass," said Gary Canant, "but they still kept coming."

"Lt. Joyner ran from hole to hole as it got underway," added Spindler, "directing fire when the perimeter was breached."

Highly respected artillery forward observer LCpl Paul McHenry fell from an incoming RPG. Gravely wounded, he managed to call for the pre-plotted Final Protective Fire before he died.

Lance Corporal Paul McHenry

By 0635, the enemy had occupied about five Lima Company fighting holes. From the command post, located in a bomb crater about 40 meters from the breach in Lima's lines, Capt. Austin directed Joyner to organize a counterassault force of all available Marines to re-take the positions now occupied by the enemy. In the din of battle, the word spread to "fix bayonets and be careful who you are shooting at."

Joyner collected about a dozen Marines, including rifleman Gary Maxwell. At the same time, Joyner directed the right guide, Cpl. Ozzie Carriman, to muster all available Marines for the assault group. "One Marine rifleman refused to move from his fighting position," said Maxwell, telling Carriman he had "only 14 days left in-country and was too short for this shit."

With no time to argue, Joyner led the counterattack of Marines on-line, horizontal to the direction of advance.

"Lt. Joyner was very brave," said Maxwell "He re-grouped us and provided leadership to re-take our lines and thereby prevented total disaster."

Mike Talley, a machine gunner, noticed Joyner leading his small band of Marines on his right flank about 15 feet away, firing and maneuvering down the slope in a counter-attack toward the enemy-occupied fighting positions.

Talley fired his machine gun at the enemy and paused. To his right he saw Joyner throw himself down on the ground. But, after a few seconds and without warning, as if the lieutenant had seen something move down the hill ahead of him, he stood back up near Tally's position. Joyner fired a single shot from his .45

pistol. Almost at the same time, an enemy volley struck him in the head and he fell.

In a fighting hole just 20 feet away, Maxwell also saw the lieutenant hit, but had to continue the counterattack. By 0730, after fierce close-in fighting, the Marines had regained their lines, expelling all positions occupied by the enemy. Although sporadic fighting would continue until mid-afternoon, the breach had been eliminated.

The NVA attack on Hill 658 and its aftermath left 19 Marines dead, 77 wounded, and one missing in action. The dead included Lt. Stephen Douglass Joyner.

"It was apparent Lt. Joyner had been shot through the head by most likely an AK-47-round and died instantly without pain," said Maxwell. "I helped carry his body up the hill to the battalion aid station where the chaplain gave him Last Rites."

Fourteen

THE RETURN

On 18 June 1968, Marine Corps casualty officers noti-fied June Joyner of her son's death. The mother and two sisters—Kaaren and June Ann—were overtaken by sudden and horrific grief. As the news spread, relatives and friends throughout California and the nation were shocked and heartbroken.

"I don't know a boy I'm closer to," Hal Sherbeck, Steve's old JC football coach told a reporter from the Fullerton newspaper. "This is like losing a son of my own. He had such great faith in America . . ."

That was echoed by Bill Wheeler, a close family friend and Exalted Ruler of the Fullerton Elks' Lodge, who openly pon-dered "why a man of this caliber is taken in the prime of his life?"

"Stephen was like a son to me," he said. "We spent many hours together. The loss of his father was a subject of constant conversation. His love for his mother is beyond expression. Words cannot express his devotion to his sisters. His patriotism to his country is unchallenged."

LT. STEPHEN JOYNER
1944 - 1968

In tribute to Lt. Stephen Joyner. U.S.M.C. our Brother, who asked not what his country could do for him . . . but instead, gave his last full measure of devotion for our country.

Khe Sahn, Vietnam -- June 15, 1968

Cover of the *Hilltop Bugle*, the Fullerton Elks Lodge No. 1993

Down at San Diego State, Steve's fraternity dealt with both grief and turmoil, a few of the brothers who backed the war effort angrily suggesting to some who opposed the war that they had better not attend the funeral or there would be trouble. Out of respect for the family, some stayed home.

Amidst the grief, hundreds of condolences poured in to the Joyner family.

Most thoughts and prayers came from those who knew Steve—family, childhood friends, football teammates, fraternity brothers, schoolmates, and Marines. Some of the letters were from government officials at all levels, from California politicians to the President of the United States. Others came from members of civic organizations.

"Knowing him personally, we realize how much he shall be missed and mourned in the community for which he has done so much," wrote Stephen Borak on behalf of the Orange County American Legion. "We are grieved beyond expression . . . God bless and comfort you."

Sam Yorty, the Mayor of Los Angeles, knew June Joyner through her work on the state school board and Steve for helping on a past campaign. "I am extremely sorry," wrote Yorty. "He was a wonderful young man."

"He was such a good son and human being," wrote Ida Brodie Arestad, Mayor Yorty's aide. "My thoughts have been with you as well as my prayers."

Stephen Joyner's body arrived at a Fullerton mortuary on 28 June. His mother requested that he be buried in his officers' dress whites, but when the uniform was not available, he was placed in his dress blues.

Lt. Joyner casket

On 1 July, the funeral service was held at the First Friends Church of Yorba Linda. The *Fullerton News-Tribune*—under the headline "War Hero"—would report that "downtown Yorba Linda was choked with automobiles . . . crowds of people stood outside because the church was filled."

Friends Church pastor H. Glen Shaffer, a close friend and mentor to Steve, conducted the service.

"We meet today in loving memory of Lt. Stephen Joyner," Shaffer began. "Born October 26, 1943 in Hollywood,

California, he gave his life for his country near Khe Sanh, Vietnam, June 15, 1968."

Pastor Shaffer admitted that "a eulogy would embarrass Stephen, but it is good for us to remember the caliber of this young man."

The pastor mentioned Steve's many gifts and the naturalness that made him so easy to know and be around. He emphasized that Lt. Joyner "loved his country and his Marine Corps." He proclaimed that the young man had answered the Christian prayer for "men to match our mountains." He noted, "Stephen's love for Christ, his country and his family were strong. In a day when thoughtfulness for parents is almost passé, he excelled. . . ."

Pastor Shaffer concluded the eulogy with a Bible verse that a man "in Christ becomes a new creation, old things are passed away, behold all things become new." (Note: the entire eulogy appears in Appendix A).

According to high school football teammate Pat Moretta, the many attendees at the funeral included at least four former girlfriends, each of whom thought at some point that she had a shot at becoming Mrs. Steve Joyner. The ladies compared notes after the memorial service, and despite the tearful occasion, tried to find some humor and comfort in the fact that each cared so much for him.

Stephen Joyner was laid to rest, next to his father, and later his mother, at Loma Vista Memorial Cemetery with full military honors.

Fifteen

Aftermath

In September 1968, I returned home from 13 months in Vietnam. I was 23 years old, my first mission: to pay a condolence visit to Steve Joyner's mother at her Fullerton apartment. While apprehensive about the visit, I did not anticipate the strained and silent reception from Mrs. Joyner, Steve's younger sister June Ann, and family relative Charles Warren. I explained as best I could how I came to know Steve, how we had met in Okinawa and had become friends. Hoping it would reassure them, I related the warm comments that he had made to me about his family. I expressed my heartfelt sympathy on the loss of a good and honorable man with unlimited promise in life.

The family met my comments with grim, quiet acknowledgement. The deep pain and understandable anger in their loss made an indelible impression. Four months after Steve's passing, the Joyner family struggled to comprehend what had happened to him and why. I sensed they wondered, perhaps with some resentment, how and why a friend of Stephen's from Vietnam had made it back while he had not.

After a few awkward moments, Charles Warren responded with halting anguish that the family had at first refused to believe the notification that Stephen had died in combat. The Marine Corps had shipped his remains to California with the recommendation that the funeral be conducted in closed casket. Against the advice of the Marine casualty officers who handled the case, the family demanded the coffin be opened for Warren to identify the body. At the mortuary, Warren said, he found it difficult to identify Stephen, his head wrapped in bandages. Then he found a childhood scar.

After another long period of silence, Stephen's mother spoke. "What should I do with his uniforms?" I hesitated, not confident of what to say to relieve her pain. Perhaps she might consider donating or selling them on consignment to the Uniform Shop at Camp Pendleton Marine Corps Base. Mrs. Joyner expressed disgust with the options, saying she would not give away the uniforms; neither would she sell them.

By the end of my hour-long visit, the family had opened up, relaxed, and seemed to appreciate my visit.

What I had not told them that day was the truth about how Steve's death had affected me. The loss of my two closest friends in Vietnam—Ken Stetson and Steve Joyner—had been pivotal events affecting my personal view of the war. Losing them hollowed me out emotionally. It seemed to take nearly everything out of me. I felt like a dead man walking the rest of my tour. Although I strived to encourage and motivate my Marines while performing my duties as XO of my artillery battery, I struggled to conceal my sense of loss. When I met with Steve's family, I had the last known letter that he had written, dated 8 June, one week before his death. I gave a copy to Mrs. Joyner.

Big Dan-

Thanks for the great pictures and the info. You talk about incoming! Let me tell you what we received in the last 24 hrs. Within our company perimeter over 126 82mm mortar rounds. The Arty battery at Khe Sanh, which I don't know off hand, really gives us support, e.g. H and I (Harassment and Interdiction—random fires on possible enemy positions) at night and an 8" gun for close support!

We are still at 689, approx. 4,000 meters west of Khe Sanh. No word when we will leave . . . I hope soon.

The weather is still very humid & hot . . . today 107. Chow still C-rats. Our SPs (special food rations) sure help.

I am commanding officer till our new skipper comes. Capt. McLaughlin rotated on 24 May. The Colonel has informed me his relief should be in-country around mid-June. At any rate, the experience is something else. Last night alone I had NDF (Night Defensive Fires) called into our area and the lines went 100% (alert). All-in-all, I love it, you know that.

Well buddy, I might see you in Australia in July. That is where I am going. Let me know your dates ASAP.

Thanks again for the pictures.

Two months after I visited June Joyner's home in La Habra, she sent me a newspaper clipping that had a photo of the family receiving her son's posthumous award for bravery, the Bronze Star with "Combat V."

Third Battalion Fourth Marines had initiated a posthumous combat award three days after the lieutenant's death. It began as a draft for a Navy Achievement Medal written by Capt. Carr. However, after further input from various command staffs and recommendations signifying Joyner's heroic actions in helping save the lives of wounded Marines during combat action, the commanding general of the Fleet Marine Force Pacific did the right thing and approved an upgrade of the award.

In September 1968, U.S. Marine Commandant Leonard F. Chapman notified June Joyner that her son had received the Bronze Star Medal with Combat "V".

"I know you will cherish this award which has been made in recognition of your son's meritorious service in combat," added General Chapman. "The Marine Corps shares your pride in the memory of your son as a gallant Marine."

Condolences regarding Steve's death continued for months, honors for years. Along with an academic scholarship, the

Fullerton Junior College Foundation created the Lt. Stephen D. Joyner Memorial Football Award. By design, it is awarded each year to one or two football players planning to transfer as eligible juniors to a four-year institution. The recipients must possess "in good measure the traits of loyalty, sportsmanship, leadership, citizenship and personal warmth that characterized the man memorialized by the award."

On the campus at San Diego State University, Stephen Douglass Joyner's name is engraved on a large, permanent memorial dedicated to former students who lost their lives in war.

In the mid-eighties, when Don Coryell was the head coach of the San Diego Chargers, he was asked privately by sportswriter and Joyner fraternity brother Bob Gaines about his former defensive end. Coryell stopped, seemingly staring across the empty football field, tears welling in his eyes.

"Steve Joyner played football . . . life . . . with all his heart and soul," said an emotional Coryell. "I loved that guy."

Retired Marine colonel Ross Brown, another San Diego State graduate, also had the chance to ask Coach Coryell many years later about Joyner. Coryell, eyes once again unable to hide his sorrow, affirmed that he fondly remembered the "quality kid."

In June 2007, Steve was inducted into the Fullerton Junior College Athletic Hall of Fame. At the banquet, retired football coach Hal Sherbeck cried as he read the induction biography. As the ceremony concluded, attendees approached Kaaren and thanked her for her brother's sacrifice. One person told her that Steve had been the best player who had ever attended FJC. Another said that she believed Steve was there that night at the banquet and that he was in a safe place. On Kaaren's program, Coach Sherbeck wrote a personal note to Steve under his photograph:

"You are and have been the greatest. Your life has and always will be one I will never forget. Our talks and your comment to someday come and work for me was a great reward. I will always remember our lives together. Your old coach, Hal Sherbeck."

Sixteen

FIFTY YEARS ON

It has been nearly half a century since Steve Joyner lost his life in Vietnam. But time has not dimmed the memories or vanquished the sorrow that followed. Friends and family continue to mourn what might have been. How and why did this generous spirit make such an indelible impression on so many people?

During the fateful siege of 15 June 1968, Lt. Joyner had moved near machine gunner Mike Talley. The enemy volley that took Steve's life, Talley has always believed, had in fact been aimed at his machine gun position.

John Hudson was with the lieutenant when Lima Company landed on Hill 658. "I've thought about that day and that week thousands of times," said Hudson. "That one week at Phou Nhoi still haunts me. Lt. Joyner was a brave man who gave his life to his country. He was a hero."

Jim Day was more than the platoon leader who preceded Joyner at Lima Company. They would become the closest of friends. "I am honored to have served with him," Day wrote.

John Seebold, a Marine veteran and fraternity brother at San Diego State, played an instrumental role in creating a plaque that hangs at Sigma Phi Epsilon. "I know for certain that we never lose the people we love, even to death," wrote Seebold in a tribute to Joyner. "They continue to participate in every act, thought and decision we make. Their love leaves an indelible imprint in our memories. We find comfort in knowing that our lives have been enriched by having shared their love."

Former Fullerton JC athletic trainer Bill Chambers treasured the time spent with Joyner. "When God created him, He destroyed the mold," said Chambers, noting that Steve was a "giant among men, his personality made him bigger than life."

Ken Kruschke, who had been a Lima Company corpsman, remembered that the Marines who served under Lt. Joyner loved him because he first and foremost cared about them. "Whatever he told you," said Kruschke, "it was true and came from his heart."

Skip Sims last saw Joyner at OCS graduation in 1966. "He still wears his warm, generous smile in my memory," Sims recalled. "I think that news of his death in Vietnam affected me more than any of the other bad news from that war. If I ever get to the Vietnam Veterans Memorial, Steve's engraved name will be the first I touch and the first one I trace."

Panel 57W at the Vietnam Veterans Memorial on
the National Mall, Washington, D.C.

Remembrances have been left at two websites dedicated to servicemen lost in the Vietnam War. These honest and heart-felt tributes, as much as anything else, provide eloquent testimony to the deep impressions Steve left with his friends and colleagues. Basic School classmate Jack Kaminski, who shared Joyner's BOQ room with him, noted that as years have passed, he often thinks of Steve. On visits to the Vietnam Veterans' Memorial, Kaminski sometimes leaves notes or flowers for him on the 57W panel that includes his name.

The following lightly edited memorials have been left at the Vietnam Veterans Virtual Wall and the Vietnam Veterans Memorial websites:

Mike Reilly was a classmate and friend with Lt. Joyner at The Basic School:

> "In Heaven there is no Beer—Steve, we used to sing that song when drinking beer at Dong Ha. It always makes me remember you. Have thought about you many times over these years that have passed. Hope to see you in heaven and have a beer too! Semper Fi." – Mike Reilly (Feb 1, 2007)

Machine gun squad leader Gary Saucier of Lima Company was with Joyner on Hill 658 the day he died. "I took all his gear and wore it the rest of my tour," said Saucier. "I knew him a brief time, but I felt like I knew him for a lot longer. I don't know why his death bothered me so much more than the others, but it still bothers me today. I can still see me carrying him to the chopper and watching until it went out of sight. It has stuck in my mind for all this time."

Saucier left a message at The Wall:

> "Friend/Soldier/Hero—1st Lt. Stephen Joyner was a friend, a leader, and a fine Marine. He saved a lot of lives including mine. He had compassion for his men. He treated everyone like a man, instead of some fighting machine. I was proud to serve with him and fight alongside of him. After Lt. Joyner died, I helped put him on a chopper and I carried his helmet and his cartridge belt for the

rest of the time I was in Vietnam. I will never forget him as long as I shall live. God rest his soul!" – Gary Saucier, Friend/Machine gun Squad Leader [Aug 17, 2000]

Two months later, Saucier returned to The Wall on what would have been Steve Joyner's 57th birthday:

"I just wanted to say Happy Birthday Lieutenant. You are always in my thoughts." – Gary Saucier [October 26, 2000]

J.R. Spindler, an S-2 Scout with Lima Company on Hill 658, had also been with Lt. Joyner the day he died.

"Two nights before, Steve told me he intended to extend in Nam in order to be promoted to captain. He had decided to make the Marine Corps his career. He was a fine officer and took his duty seriously. He was level headed and protected his troops up to the day he died. I probably owe my life to him. I think of him often and can only hope he has found peace through the Grace of God." – Jules Spindler [6 Sept 2001]

Joe Gerry had been a friend of Steve's at San Diego State and was in the same Basic School platoon:

"A Friend, Fellow Marine—Lt. Joyner and I went to the same college and trained in the same Basic School class. He was known as a leader before he was a Marine. I honor his sacrifice and remember him every day." – Joe Gerry, 1st Lt. USMC, Retired [Oct 26, 2000]

As a young girl, Laurie Johnson had sent Steve a care package from the states which he had graciously shared with his company.

"I was a Girl Scout in 1968. Our troop, under my mother's leadership, sent care packages to the soldiers in Vietnam. My package went to Lt. Stephen Joyner. I didn't know how lucky I was that it went to him. He sent me the kindest thank you note I have ever received. He told me about himself and about his plans. We found out he had been killed a few weeks after I received the letter. It broke my heart and had a profound effect on me. I still have the letter and often wonder what would have become of him. He was really a good man." – Laurie Johnson [29 April 2008]

Stephen Joyner's family experienced an immeasurable void with his loss and surviving members still feel the pain. During a 2014 conversation, Gil Warren choked back tears, saying his cousin's death devastated the family. Warren had learned of Steve's death reading the *Stars and Stripes* newspaper in Korea. June Joyner gave her son's highly polished black dress shoes to him. The shoes sit, untouched, always visible, in Warren's closet.

June Joyner never fully recovered from the loss of her son. She remarried in the 1970s and went on to have a short civil service career with the Post Office. Years later, she and Kaaren mused with some levity—infused perhaps with hope—that a "little Steve Joyner" might be running around Vietnam or elsewhere.

When Kaaren and Ernie Page had twins, they named one of the boys Stephen. Decades later, in reading one of her brother's letters for the first time, Kaaren learned that one day he wanted a son named Douglass and a daughter named Janice Marie. Seeing his words caused yet another emotional, bittersweet moment for Kaaren . . . her middle name is Marie.

Steve's younger sister, June Anne Person, and her husband are settled in Alaska.

———

No one can say of course with any certainty the path that Steve Joyner's life might have taken had he survived Vietnam. From accounts of Marines who spoke with him days before he died, he had decided to pursue a career with the Marines. We know that at the end of May 1968, he had initiated the paperwork required for augmentation into the regular Marine Corps. He may or may not have been selected as a career Marine officer. If he had made the Marine Corps a career, he doubtless would have been the compassionate leader that some of his senior officers in Vietnam were not.

Had his plans for a career in the Marines changed for any reason, coaching football seemed to be an obvious option for him. His involvement in strong football programs at both Fullerton and San Diego State—and the close relationships he established with the coaching staffs there—pointed in that direction. Respected and valued by coaches at both institutions, one can readily imagine that Steve would have been hired as an assistant at either school. A San Diego State teammate who went into football coaching himself postulated that had Steve become a coach, he would have changed many lives for the better. It is impossible to argue otherwise.

Unique qualities of character made Joyner a memorable man. He believed in the best of people. He often accepted at face value what others told him. His strong family values and organized football experience and its culture loomed large in shaping who he became. This carried over to the Marine Corps. He adhered to his belief systems formed at a young age, shaped by his parents, and developed further by his football coaches over the years. Joyner continually grew in his religious faith.

He believed totally in the principles of the organizations in which he participated—football with its emphasis on determination and teamwork, public service in community organizations such as the Elks, and the Marine Corps with its discipline, esprit de corps, and commitment to higher ideals. He thought the transition from the values and culture of college football to those of the Marine Corps would be a natural transition for him. He believed in the purpose of all his endeavors.

Steve approached life and work at full tilt, with no compromises. He embraced patriotism, love of country, and a firm belief in God. He found it difficult sometimes to comprehend why others did not share his values and enthusiasm.

He treated friends, fellow officers, and his enlisted Marines with complete respect. Void of ego himself, and with the awareness that no human being was perfect, he refused to criticize others. Rather, he sought to encourage and support everyone.

He looked to the positive side of life. From childhood to the Marine Corps, he possessed an irrepressible optimism, cheerfulness, and can-do attitude. He worked hard to be the best person and officer he could be. He sought with joy to do the right thing.

His character and integrity did not change in the crucible of Vietnam. He was true to himself and his values. He retained his humanity and sustained efforts to support his fellow Marines. The eloquent simplicity and testaments of the memorials from those who knew and worked with him speak for themselves.

Stephen Joyner venerated family bonds and relationships. In many ways, he embodied the values of a loving family environment that encouraged hard work and honest living. He would have been a dedicated husband and father. He would have mentored others. "Togetherness" was a word he used often when communicating with family.

Our world is diminished by his absence and his promise lost.

Appendix A

LETTERS AND HONORS

Following are a few documents that were briefly discussed within the book.

Loving Parents (1946)

To celebrate their fifth anniversary, Steve (the dad) wrote a love letter to June:

This isn't anything fancy because I'm not that way. I thought about a card, but I thought instead I'd write a letter of my own.

We have really come a long way, in my estimation, from a day five years ago when you had the courage and intestinal fortitude to say "I do" to a character like me with only 75 cents to my name and not even knowing where my next nickel was coming from.

You have been wonderful through ruff (sic) times and through good times. When I need you, you are always there as the one to make even the darkest situation seem bright and gay.

You have given birth to two of the most wonderful, intelligent, and best looking children. You have been a wonderful mother, and we have every right to be so proud of them. They have made a wonderful dream come true for me.

It is also a wonderful feeling to have a few bonds, a little money in my pocket and be free of debt. My only debt is to you, which I could never repay for all the wonderful moments you have given me.

So let me take this opportunity to tell you, that in all my travels, from coast to coast and border to border, averaging 75,000 miles per year, I have never met, in all my travels, a person with a more likeable personality; a better looking; a better built; a better sport or truer companion; and a prouder husband no woman ever had than you – my Darling True Wife -

"Steve"

A Legendary Coach (1963)

San Diego State coach Don Coryell urges Steve to remain at Fullerton JC for his sophomore football season rather than transfer to a four-year school:

Please remember, Steve, that your education is the most important thing in your life at this time. By staying at Fullerton fall semester and then coming to San Diego State for five more semesters, you will have an excellent education, an extra year of schooling, and three years of football instead of two seasons.

In many ways our financial aid program is better than the official NCAA scholarship.

Our football program is on the way up – by the time you graduate, we plan to be able to hold our own with the major colleges in the nation. Our schedule is improving.

Steve, I want you and your mother and father to come to our campus for a visit. I would like to take you and your folks out to dinner. Your mother and dad may have some questions to ask me.

Don Coryell, Head Football Coach

To Stetson's Wife (1968)

I wrote the following letter to Ken Stetson's wife, Jan, three weeks after his loss during the Battle for Hue and several days after I arrived in Okinawa for Embarkation School. The qualities that I found in Stetson were discussed with Steve Joyner. Jan Stetson Boespflug would remarry and raise a family. Forty-seven years later after Ken's death, Jan sent me a copy of the letter:

7 March 1968, Thursday

Dear Mrs. Stetson,

I have delayed in writing you because I wanted the time to think and choose the words that could express what I want to say to you in your time of extreme sorrow.

Your husband and I worked together on a forward observer team from August to early January (1967). On 3 January I left Golf Company and LCpl Stetson took over the team. I think that I knew him as well as anyone here.

We had several long conversations over the months. We were as close to one another as an officer and enlisted man could be, I suppose. I had great respect for him and believe he felt the same about me.

I could go into detail about how well liked and admired he was by the entire Echo Battery and Golf Company. I know that you have received other letters expressing this fact and it should make you proud.

I cannot write, however, without intimating to you what he meant to me. His death is a great personal loss to me and I admit that a void has appeared that will never be filled.

I tried very hard to teach him everything I had learned in artillery school. I took pride in the knowledge that I had the best FO I could possibly have. I trained him not only because I knew that someday I would leave the team and return to the battery and other duties, but because he was exceptionally receptive to learning as much as possible. He was professional, and by his nature, he could not help but be a friend to me. He was a Marine with no pretensions, and uncommonly good person.

He was the ideal combat Marine. He was a generous spirit, bigger than life. He freely gave of himself.

I talked with the Golf Company Commander about him briefly during the lull in the fight for Hue. Captain Meadows mentioned your husband's exemplary conduct during the strain of combat, how he stood watches for his fellow Marines and did his best to lighten the mental and physical burden of others without regard to his own comforts. I am afraid my words cannot do justice to the deep respect I had for him.

He continually gave of himself, an unselfishness that will serve as an outstanding example for all who knew him.

With Sincere Sympathy and Regards,

Dan Moore

Patriotic Letter to Elks (1968)

Disturbed by a growing anti-war sentiment at home, Lt. Joyner wrote of his frustrations and hopes in a letter to the Fullerton Elks:

Dear Brother Elks:

Hello from Hill 689, Khe Sanh, South Viet Nam. I am fine except for the extreme heat and humidity. Today it was 107.

My purpose in writing is to express my viewpoints on a very meaningful subject to me and I know that it is important to you too. In a recent 'Stars and Stripes' newspaper, I read an article on patriotism. The article was from an interview which took place on one of our state college campuses. The entire article never once mentioned the idea that patriotism is what makes our country strong. It provides cohesiveness to an amalgamation of people unlike that of any other country in the world.

The Vietnam conflict has developed strong feelings within me and I would like to pass on my viewpoints to you.

Is Patriotism a dirty word?

It's not a dirty word to a young Marine sitting in the mud near the Demilitarized Zone.

It's not a dirty word to a fighter pilot floating in the Gulf of Tonkin waiting to be rescued.

It's not a dirty word to people who compile dictionaries – who define patriotism with words like love and loyal or zealous support of one's own country.

Patriotism is what makes our country strong. It provides the substance through which the lives, hopes, and desires of all American citizens are fulfilled.

Then why do so many Americans seem ashamed of the word? Why do so many of them apologize for their country in speeches, written articles, and through dubious demonstrations? Why do they hide the word and the ideas of patriotism? Why do they call patriotism 'an archaic expression of nationalism'?

Nathan Hale didn't apologize for his country as he was about to be hanged. Why should you apologize because loving your country gives you a feeling of satisfaction?

We're proud of being called patriots. It labels us loyal defenders of our country and its ideals. It's a good thing to have this feeling. It helps you to hold your head up high. It makes your country beautiful and you can feel this beauty. It makes you a better citizen. And if you are a better citizen, your country has to be the ultimate beneficiary.

Let's tell people about patriotism. They'll understand. They might even get to like the idea . . . all of them.

I hope this letter finds you all in good health and spirits.

— Stephen D Joyner, USMC

Eulogy for Stephen Douglass Joyner (1968)

On 1 July, the First Friends Church of Yorba Linda held the Funeral Service for Lieutenant Stephen Joyner. The text of Pastor H. Glen Shaffer's eulogy:

We meet today in loving memory of Lt. Stephen Joyner. Born October 26, 1943 in Hollywood, California, he gave his life for his country near Khe Sanh, Vietnam, June 15th, 1968.

A eulogy would embarrass Stephen. But it is good for us to remember the caliber of this young man. We dare not forget the price that some men and families pay to keep our country free.

As a Christian young man with many gifts, he had a naturalness that made him an easy person to know and be around. He graduated from La Habra High School in 1961, from Fullerton

JC in 1964, and from San Diego State in 1966. Football was one of Stephen's great loves. In 1962 he was All Eastern Conference defensive end, and was also selected on the first string All American team in 1963 before he graduated from JC. He also received the Art Nunn Award as the outstanding athlete of the year.

Stephen loved his country and his Marine Corps. Writing from Hill 689 in a letter to the Fullerton Elks Lodge, he expressed his positive views on patriotism. He asked, is patriotism a dirty word? It's not. Let's tell people about patriotism."

Some of you will remember this headline on the sports page of the *LA Times*, Oct 6, 1963:

Choir Boy . . . tough guy on College Gridiron . . . "Steve Joyner is a choir boy, but he doesn't play football like one. He spends the first part of his weekends taking apart the opposition on the gridiron and the second part singing with the College Young Friends . . . And one night a month the group conducts a worship service at Orange County jail."

While still in high school, Stephen learned an important truth about life that some people never learn. He discovered that man was made for God, and that life has meaning when it is lived to glorify Jesus Christ.

Stephen's love for Christ, his country and his family were strong. In a day when thoughtfulness for parents is almost passé, he excelled in his thoughtfulness.

Someone has prayed for "Men to match our mountains." Lt. Stephen Joyner was an answer to this prayer. In his 24 years, he lived more than most people will live in 75 years. As his JC coach said, Steve gave 110 percent."

In his last letter to this church that he loved, written 28 April, the salutation said "To all my wonderful friends . . . a warm hello." He closed that letter by saying: "I send my prayers of you and our church," Signed, "In his Name . . . Stephen".

What great assurance we have because Stephen could sign his letter as a man "in Christ's name." What great confidence Stephen had because of his faith in Christ. The New Testament tells us that a man "in Christ becomes a new creation, old things are passed away, behold all things become new."

Memorial Letter from the Elks (1968)
Written by BillWheeler, the Exalted Ruler of the Fullerton Elks, this letter appeared in the July 1968 issue of The Hilltop Bugle, *the official publication for Lodge No. 1993:*

In mid-February 1965 we brothers of the Elks suffered a tragedy in the loss of our Ex-Exalted Ruler Homer Joyner. Tonight we pay tribute to another brother, 1st Lt Stephen Joyner, USMC, son of the deceased Ex-Exalted Ruler of 1964-1965.

Lt. Joyner joined the lodge Dec 3, 1964 shortly after his 21st birthday, his father being the officiating officer.

What is an Elk? A member who follows the principles of our order: charity, justice, brotherly love and fidelity. There is little need for me to elaborate on Lt. Joyner's fulfillment of the principles of our obligation to this fine organization.

His love for the United States is far beyond reproach. In fact, he volunteered for Vietnam. In the first place, being the only surviving male of a family, he was under no obligation to go to Vietnam.

Stephen in his many visits to my home was in the process of making a plaque. On the plaque was his Dad's photograph, [inscribed] Exalted Ruler 1964-1965, with the Elk's emblem. One of Stephen's greatest desires was eventually to be Exalted Ruler of this Lodge.

If all our citizens were of the caliber of our deceased brother our United States would have more pride and have more respect in the world community.

A Second Letter to Ken Stetson's Wife (1969)

After my return from Vietnam, on the first anniversary of Ken Stetson's death—17 February 1969—I wrote a second letter to his wife, Jan, trying to express again what her husband had meant to me:

Dear Mrs. Stetson,

I am writing to answer a few questions which you asked me nearly a year ago. It was a year ago today that Kenneth died. I do not want to renew a grief, rather try to put you at peace. I did not answer your March letter immediately for several reasons I can't explain.

I hope this past year hasn't been a lost one for you. An empty one in many respects, to be sure, but I trust you have found new hope in the future.

Kenneth and hundreds like him could not ask for any more than to be remembered by the ones they loved. I guess that is as much as we can do, helpless though it seems.

Kenneth lived about three hours after being shot but was not in much pain because of sedatives and other medication. He did begin dictating a letter to you but it was only a few words long.

What more I can relate concerns only his sacrifice and devotion to duty.

I sincerely wish you the best life offers in the future.

Fullerton JC Prominent Alumni (2013)

In its centennial year of 2013, Fullerton College named Stephen Joyner as one its prominent alumni:

Stephen Joyner was an All-Conference end for the Hornet Football teams. He was a 1st team Junior College All-American selection as a sophomore, and led the Hornets to the Eastern Conference Championship. Joyner was further honored as the recipient of the Arthur L. Nunn Memorial Award presented to the "Most Inspirational Athlete" of the 1964-65 year. Joyner's selection of this award was based on his inspirational leadership qualities, his athletic success, and his academic success. He was also selected as one of 25 top Fullerton College campus "Men of Distinction" in 1964.

Joyner transferred to San Diego State for his upper-division work, and continued his football career with two outstanding seasons as an Aztec. Following graduation, Stephen enlisted in the U.S. Marine Corps, and was commissioned as an officer [in 1966]. While serving his country as a combat officer, Lt. Stephen Joyner was killed in action on June 15, 1968.

A scholarship fund was set up . . . to honor Lt. Stephen Joyner's outstanding service to his country, his community, and to Fullerton College.

Sigma Phi Epsilon Plaque and Tribute (2014)

Fraternity brother John Seebold created a plaque in memory of Steve that hangs in the Sig Ep house at San Diego State University. Seebold— himself a Marine who had been wounded at Khe Sanh in 1968—recently wrote some thoughts about his fallen brother:

Of thee I sing.

There are many callings in every society. Of these paths, the path of the warrior is one of the more difficult. You were called upon to fight for others' safety and freedom, knowing that this path may include giving your life and the suffering of your loved ones.

The path requires courage, commitment, and resilience. The courage to face the brutality of war, the commitment to leave behind loved ones and the resilience to keep your humanity in the face of inhumanity are the mark of a true warrior. You understood duty and honor, and never flinched when your country called. You knew the cost of war and the sacrifice that must be made for freedom. Freedom is not free, and the price of freedom always will be the blood of a warrior.

Through your actions and sacrifice, we enjoy the blessings of liberty and freedom. Always, my deepest gratitude and respect.

Semper Fidelis. Steve, being a Marine, these words and only these words are the final words he may have uttered. This was a pragmatic and capable man.

I know for certain that we never lose the people we love, even to death. They continue to participate in every act, thought and decision we make. Their love leaves an indelible imprint in our memories. We find comfort in knowing that our lives have been enriched by having shared their love.

So it is, death leaves a heartache no one can heal, love leaves a memory no one can steal. Our friendship was truly a treasured one. It was like a river flowing over rocks that form the basement of time. On top of the rocks are the raindrops of our experiences and under the rocks are the words. We were not of the same blood, but of a different family. A Marine family joined by circumstance and held together by respect. What Steve did in his life makes him larger than life. His essence, spirit, and courage will be immortalized by those who honor his memory . . . and it will last forever . . .

Appendix B

ACKNOWLEDGEMENTS

First, I wish to acknowledge and thank my wife, Patricia Moore, who served as an expert advisor throughout the inception, research, organization, and writing of the Stephen Joyner story. Her advice, comments, edits and overall infallible judgment proved crucial, as did her accomplished IT skills. She knew for years the importance that I placed on recording Steve's journey through life and did all she could to help see it through to completion. I could not have finished the project without her support and assistance.

The Joyner project began in earnest in the summer of 2014 after conversations with Wake Forest University professor Al Claiborne, whose cousin, Norman A. Lane, served with Steve Joyner at TBS, the U.S. Naval Base in Guantanamo and with Third Battalion Fourth Marines (3/4). Professor Claiborne encouraged me to proceed with the research and provided contact information of Marines who served in 3/4 at various times during Joyner's tour in Vietnam.

Former Third Battalion Fourth Marines Forward Observer Michael Madden generously provided assistance early on, putting me in contact with many Marines in the battalion who had served with Lt. Joyner. He also facilitated my contact with Steve's sister, Kaaren Joyner Page.

From the outset, Kaaren was the key person who drove my research. She provided dozens of letters her brother had written to her and his mother while he served in Vietnam and she brokered my contacts with numerous family relatives and friends who knew him well. She provided key information on the Joyner family and Steve's early life and later obtained Lt. Joyner's personnel records from the U.S. Marine Corps, which added critical detail on his various assignments. Kaaren provided family photos and an illuminating scrapbook she kept of Steve's exploits on the gridiron. Her email responses to specific questions filled in many gaps. Meetings with her in San Diego and McLean, Virginia further highlighted the close and loving relationship she had with her younger brother.

La Habra High School teammate Pat Moretta provided critical information about Steve's high school football career and important details on his character and views during his Vietnam tour.

Brig Owens—former Assistant Executive Director of the NFL Players Association and selected as one of the greatest players in the history of the Washington Redskins—provided valuable information on their time together as friends and teammates at Fullerton JC. Owens also put me in contact with former NFL and college coach John Pease—another teammate at FJC—and athletic trainer Bill Chambers. Brig's wife, Patti, added information on Steve's visit to Cincinnati before he committed to play football at San Diego State.

Interviews with Steve's fraternity brothers and Aztec football teammates provided informative detail about his life at San Diego State. John Seebold first put me in contact with members of Joyner's fraternity. A former Marine, Seebold read early draft chapters. Another fraternity brother, Joe Sullivan, also reviewed the draft and generously provided useful comments.

Joe Sullivan also organized my visit to the San Diego State campus, including meetings with key Alumni Office officials. Executive Director of Alumni Affairs Jim Herrick's staff identified former Aztec teammates of Steve Joyner. Alumni Affairs staff writer Tobin Vaughn published an article on the Joyner project and encouraged alumni who knew Steve to contact me.

Marine Corps friends and colleagues were key in providing perspectives of Lt. Joyner's years in the Corps and in Vietnam. I am particularly indebted to Jim Day for his observations and insights, having worked side by side with Joyner for seven months. Former Lieutenant Martin Traiser provided detail on Lima Company's operations in 1968 along with valuable photographs of the period May through June 1968 and along with John Hudson, recalled Lima Company operations. Lt. Joyner's platoon sergeant, James Ables, provided critical information on the lieutenant's service with Lima. Working through Jim Day, Ables supplied photographs and remembrances that filled in gaps.

Marian Novak (author of *Lonely Girls with Burning Eyes*) and Michael Archer (author of *A Patch of Ground: Khe Sanh Remembered*, and *The Long Goodbye: Khe Sanh Revisited*) provided valued insights and comments on a late draft. Archer also provided key maps of I Corps and the Khe Sanh region. I am also indebted to author James P. Coan for permission to use maps from *Con Thien: The Hills of Angels*.

My Basic School 3-67 classmate, retired Lieutenant General Frank Libutti, offered insightful comments on what Steve Joyner encountered in Vietnam. His own combat experiences as a platoon commander—including leadership issues—shed light on what Steve Joyner must have contended with in Lima Company 3/4.

I am grateful to Steve's many friends, relatives, and colleagues who took the time to share their memories and comments. In particular, these include:

Relatives and Family Friends
Chilstrom, Louann Chantiles
Kaukola, Allison Page – Cousin
Kling, Kjell – Cousin
Morgen, Marty – Cousin, Captain, USN (Ret.)
Mouser, Sally – Cousin

Page, Kaaren Joyner – Sister
Person, June Ann Joyner – Sister
Salant, Tani Janes, Ph.D.
Warren, Gil – Cousin
Warren, Kate – Cousin
Willis, Mel
Wilson, Sue
Wryn, Maren

La Habra High School
Cadile, Sue
DeBerry, Sally Leonard
Ericsson, Janice
Fischle, Judy
McDowell, Richard – Football
Meier, Fred, Lieutenant Colonel, USMC (Ret.), also OCS
Moretta, Pat – Football
Ornelas, Barbara Anderson
Salant, Tani Janes, Ph.D.
Sutton, Jim – Football
Veatch, David – Football

Fullerton Junior College
Chambers, William – Football
Owens, Brig – Football
Owens, Patricia
Pease, John – Football

San Diego State

Biondo, Vince – Sigma Phi Epsilon

Brown, Ross, Colonel, USMC (Ret.), also OCS

Climie, Joanne

Contreras, Hil – Sigma Phi Epsilon

Duke, Alan – Football

Gaines, Bob – Sigma Phi Epsilon

Gerry, Joe – Captain, USMC, also TBS

Gerry, Michael

Gibbs, Bob – Sigma Phi Epsilon

Gillespie, Dena Windsor

Hills, Wes – Sigma Phi Epsilon

Hood, Bob – Sigma Phi Epsilon

Kinney, Cliff – Football

Ornelas, Daniel – Sigma Phi Epsilon

Seebold, John – Sigma Phi Epsilon

Sorem, Richard – Sigma Phi Epsilon

Sullivan, Joseph – Sigma Phi Epsilon

Zajonc, Robert – Sigma Phi Epsilon

U.S. Marine Corps

Ables, James, Sergeant Major, USMC (Ret.) – Lima Co.

Alton, Tracy, former Captain, USMCR

Archer, Michael – author, *A Patch of Ground: Khe Sanh Remembered* and *The Long Goodbye: Khe Sanh Revisited*

Barnas, Bob – Third Battalion Fourth Marines

Burton, Paul – Third Battalion Fourth Marines

Brown, Ross, Colonel, USMC (Ret.) – OCS
Canant, Gary – Lima Co.
Carr, John, Colonel, USMC (Ret.) – Lima Co.
Christy, Kenneth, Colonel, USMC (Ret.) – Lima Co.
Clifton, Robert – Lima Co.
Day, James C., Master Gunnery Sergeant, USMC (Ret.) – Lima Co.
Fant, Ruff – TBS
Finlayson, Andrew, Colonel, USMC (Ret.) – author, *Rice Paddy Recon* and *Killer Kane*
Fitzsimmons, Michael - TBS
Gallant, Al
Gerry, Joe, Captain, USMC – TBS
Griswold, David – TBS
Hemmert, Michael – TBS
Hofmann, George, Colonel, USMC (Ret.) – TBS
Holladay, John – Lima Co.
Hudson, John – Lima Co.
Hughey, James – TBS
Jauntig, Thomas – OCS
Johns, Al, Lieutenant Colonel, USMC (Ret.) – TBS
Johnson, Laurie – Correspondent
Jozwiakowski, Richard - TBS
Kaminski, Jack – TBS
Kelly, Sam – TBS
Kirsch, Dan - TBS
Kropp, Edward, Colonel, USMC (Ret.) – TBS

Kruschke, Ken – Lima Co.
Libutti, Frank, Lieutenant General, USMC (Ret.)
Lindsey, Edward, Lieutenant Colonel, USA (Ret.)
Madden, Michael – 3/4
Martin, Chuck – OCS
Maxwell, Gary – Lima Co.
McGinty, Jim, Colonel, USMC (Ret.) – author, *Right to Kill: A Brooklyn Tale*
Meier, Fred, Lieutenant Colonel, USMC (Ret.) – OCS
Morgan, Ron, Colonel, USMC (Ret.)
Muir, Robert, Lieutenant Colonel, USMC (Ret.)
Paull, Jerry, Lieutenant Colonel, USMC (Ret.) – TBS
Powell, John – OCS
Raper, David – Lima Co.
Ritzel, Carl - TBS
Saucier, Gary – Lima Co.
Sims, Marion "Skip" – OCS
Spindler, J.R. – H&S Co, 3/4
Swartz, Bill – OCS
Taggard, Joe – OCS
Talley, Michael – Lima Co.
Traiser, Martin – Lima Co.
Wilkerson, Leroy – OCS
Worley, Thom – Lima Co.

Photos and Maps
Page, Kaaren Joyner – Chapter 1-1, 1-2, 1-3, 1-4; 2-1; 3-2; 4-1; 5-1, 5-2; 6-1; 6-2; 9-2; 11-2; 14-2.

Fullerton Junior College – Ch. 2-2.
San Diego State University – Ch. 3-1.
Lionel Raymond – Ch. 4-2; 5-3.
James P. Coan – Ch. 7-1; 8-1; 10-1.
James Ables – Ch. 9-1; 12-3.
Ken Christy – Ch. 9-3.
Dan Moore – Ch. 11-1.
Michael Archer – Ch. 12-1.
Martin Traiser – Ch. 12-2; 13-1, 13-2, 13-3, 13-5, 13-6.
Bob Barnas – Ch. 12-4.
Paul Burton – Ch. 13-4.
Fullerton Elks Lodge No. 1993 – Ch. 14-1.
Dan Arant – Ch. 16-1.

In addition, others contributed valuable assistance to include thoughts, suggestions, input and advice as the book took shape:

Alton, Tracy, former Captain, USMCR
Archer, Michael – Vietnam veteran, author, *A Patch of Ground: Khe Sanh Remembered* and *The Long Goodbye: Khe Sanh Revisited*
Claiborne, Al – Wake Forest University
Day, James C., Master Gunnery Sergeant, USMC (Ret.)
Finlayson, Andrew, Colonel, USMC (Ret.) – author, *Rice Paddy Recon* and *Killer Kane*
Gallant, Albert – Vietnam War veteran
Heisel, Jen – SDSU, Asst. Media Relations Director
Herrick, Jim – SDSU, Asst. Vice President, Special Projects, University Relations

Kaukola, Allison – Niece
Learned, Stephen
Libutti, Frank, Lieutenant General, USMC (Ret.)
Lindsey, Edward, Lieutenant Colonel, USA (Ret.)
Maxwell, Gary – Lima Co.
Madden, Michael – 3/4
McGinty, Jim, Colonel, USMC (Ret.) – author, *Right to Kill: A Brooklyn Tale*
Morgan, Ron, Colonel, USMC (Ret.)
Muir, Robert, Lieutenant Colonel, USMC (Ret.)
Novak, Marian – author, *Lonely Girls with Burning Eyes*
Page, Kaaren Joyner – Sister
Pate, William
Paull, Jerry, Lieutenant Colonel, USMC (Ret.)
Raymond, Lionel
Richardson, John P. – author, *Alexander Robey Shepherd: The Man Who Built the Nation's Capital*
Salant, Tani Janes, Ph.D.
Sheehan, Helen, Ph.D.
Traiser, Martin – Lima Co.
Vaart, Andres, Captain, USN (Ret.) – editor, *Studies in Intelligence*
Vaughn, Tobin – SDSU writer, University Relations and Development
Wells, Bruce
Zinsmeister, Bruce
Zinsmeister, Joanne

Finally, my deepest thanks to my editor, Bob Gaines, who helped turn an overlong, ungainly manuscript into something altogether different. His constant encouragement and counsel were vital in completing this book. A former friend and fraternity brother of Steve Joyner at San Diego State, Bob wanted to get Steve's story out to the world every bit as much as I did.

Manufactured by Amazon.com
Columbia, SC
29 March 2017